A CHRISTIAN ANSWER TO
AN AGE OF NARCISSISM

It's Not About Me

DUSTIN BLUMER

DYNAMIS PUBLISHING

Published by Dynamis Publishing, in partnership with Amazon KDP.

Library of Congress Cataloging-in-Publication Data

Blumer, Dustin.
    It's Not About Me: a Christian answer to an age of narcissism/Dustin Blumer.
       pages cm
    Includes bibliographical references.
    Softcover ISBN: 9798864803035
    1. Jesus - Religious aspects - Christianity. 2. Selfishness - Religious aspects - Christianity. 3. Purpose - Religious aspects - Christianity.

Printed in the United States of America

CONTENTS

ACKNOWLEDGEMENTS

All glory be to God. He allowed the time, space, energy, and wisdom for this book.

Thank you to my family! To my wife, Kathryn, for your constant, encouraging support. To my daughters, Bella and Nadia, for your prayers, and putting up with dad. I love you!

Thank you to my church family, Amazing Love! For sharing in the excitement of this book. To our Leadership Team, for allowing time for a book to be written.

Thank you to my church staff. Courtney, I cannot thank you enough for the work you put into editing! Kristin, your thoughts on the content were so helpful!

INTRODUCTION

The ideas of this book have been in my heart and mind for quite some time. Though I applied this principle to eleven various topics - I believe it could apply to the whole of the Christian lifestyle.

The goal I had for this book is that you would be drawn closer to God, and that you would have some helpful ideas to put into practice. If you read this book and your love and awe of God grow, or you find a few helpful insights - I will consider it a win.

It's funny to me that I use personal illustrations and commentary on a book titled "It's Not About Me." Perhaps you see irony there. My hope is that as I share my experience, you see I too am humbly working this out in my own life, and that you find relatability for your own life.

The first two chapters represent the book's foundation. I would advise starting there. Chapters three through eleven can be consumed in any order after that chapters one and two. You might be more interested in one subject over another - feel free to skip to those topics. I was hoping that each chapter would have enough helpful content you wouldn't want to miss any of the chapters. Sometimes it's easy to read half-way through a book and never pick it up again.

Now may the Holy Spirit use the Word to move in your life. May this book be a blessing for you.

A prayer as you start this book: *"Heavenly Father, send your Holy Spirit that I may have eyes to see the beauty of who You are, a heart that holds You, and hands and feet that want to live out Your directives. Bless the journey I am beginning to continue to investigate how wide and long, how deep and high is Your love. Amen."*

*"Just as the Son of Man did not come to be served, **but to serve**, and to give his life as a ransom for many."*
(Matthew 20:28)

THE PROBLEM

I have a hunch the world revolves around me. I see evidence of it all the time.

In high school I was part of the graduating class of 2000. In that year, an artist known as Vitamin C released a song called "Graduation." *Of course she did,* I was graduating and come whatever I had made friends forever. When I fell in love, Enrique Iglesias wrote a perfect love song called "Escape." *Of course he did,* I was in love and this girl could run and she could hide, but she would never escape my love. When I went to Hollywood, they chose me to be a contestant on *The Price is Right.* I became BFF's with Drew Carey and won a bedroom set. *Of course again!* And because the world revolves around me I've won other things too - a Gameboy, free Raising Canes for a year, a teddy bear, and a free toothbrush from my dentist.

Because the world revolves around me, I was chosen to be a leader in the new smoke-free world. An anti-smoking campaign hinged their hopes on me as a 4th grader! *Of course they did!* I, and the rest of my class, were to be part of the smoke-free class of 2000. We had yellow T-shirts and a song with the lyrics, "We are the smoke free class of 2000. Two triple zero, everyone's a hero."[1]

Then there are religious reasons why the world revolves around me. Back in grade school, I'll never forget my moment with God. There I was in Beaver Dam, Wisconsin, observing a thunderstorm from my garage. In that moment, God told me He was returning in my lifetime. It wasn't an audible voice, just an inkling I chose to believe. I thought it was going to happen at my high school graduation when I received my diploma. It didn't happen then. But God will return in my lifetime - *of course*. God is orchestrating things around me.

More on that, I was born on Palm Sunday, and baptized on Easter. I achieved my dream of becoming a pastor after eight years of hard work studying Greek and Hebrew. I survived three years of high school Latin, and three semesters of college Latin. *Veni, Vidi, Vici!* What more evidence do you need?

Yet, if you're unconvinced about my theory that the world revolves around me....good for you. You read through the sarcasm and the bad jokes. Whose favorite love song is "Escape" anyway? That's kind of creepy. (Truth: it is our song, but only because it makes us laugh). You even learned some history about a failed attempt to make a smoke-free society.

But let me ask, have you ever thought the world revolves around you? And what evidence might you have?

Beyond pop songs, and inklings - perhaps you've experienced one of those moments when the stars aligned just for you. You were handed the keys to your dream car. You stepped across the threshold of your dream house. You heard, "I do" from the one who is your dream spouse. And along the way you also found, "Of course, the world does revolve around me!"

Still, even if you're rolling your eyes at me up to this point. Even if you are saying to yourself, "Inconceivable! No way! The world does not revolve around you or me!" I hear you. I do. It's a giant leap to believe the axis point for the world's rotation is you or me. Even putting it in those terms sounds preposterous.

Yet, here is a premise I'd like to prove: We're all pre-programmed to think "it's ALL about me."

So let me roll up my sleeves and get to work.

"Narcissist." Maybe I'm super old, but I didn't grow up with this word. I heard terms like arrogant, selfish, and egotistical. But "narcissist" was new to me. I probably don't need to do to this, but let me kick it old-school and get the definition. A narcissist is defined as "an extremely self-centered person who has an exaggerated sense of self-importance."[2] In today's world, narcissists are not novel. Narcissists are not like mystical unicorns you might see if you just look hard enough. No, narcissists are ordinary - way too ordinary.

Narcissists create havoc on the roads. They cut you off, flip you off, and honk at you, because where they are going is obviously more important than where you are going. Narcissists are found at work. They claim the credit and buck the blame. Narcissists live in our homes and neighborhoods. They destroy them. They get what they want regardless of what it means for everyone else. They cheat and lie. They let others do all the work, while blaming them for not doing it good enough. They emotionally terrorize, making everyone walk on eggshells around them. They do all of this, while remaining oblivious to the wake of hurt around them. They can't see the hurt they create, because that would mean they took the lens off of themselves.

Do you know a narcissist? And how did so many get here? Let's take a look back.

Nero was a narcissist. He burnt Rome while blaming Christians, so he could build himself a bigger palace.[3] He built a bronze statue of himself 10 stories high.[4] Hitler was a narcissist who considered himself to be part of a superior race.[5] We know the horror of where those thoughts led. Genghis Kahn was a narcissist. He had six wives and over five hundred concubines. He fathered so many children that sixteen million men or .5% of the male population today is traced back to Genghis Kahn.[6] Wow. These were next level narcissists.

What about today? We see celebrity narcissists all around us. Millions follow them on Instagram and Facebook. They have products we can buy, so we can look like them. There are political narcissists in America. Leaders who do not hold their position to represent the people, as much as their own interests. There are financial narcissists, using others so they can make more money, regardless of what this means. We saw that in the Great Recession and the banking industry. Many knew the bad loans they were writing, but didn't care because they made a buck.[7]

Yes, narcissists are all around us. And yes, I picked some pretty easy targets. But let me bring it closer.

Do you know the twelve disciples of Jesus were narcissists? Or at least, they had narcissistic tendencies. Now who am I to speak like this? I fully admit they will have better spots in heaven. They were used by God in incredible ways. Most of them died as martyrs.

Yet, they still struggled with narcissism. On more than one occasion they argued over who would be the greatest in the Kingdom of Heaven.[8] One of the more striking occasions is when Jesus had just finished washing the disciples' feet. They were in the Upper Room, and the next day He would die for them. Yet, still they argued about who would have the top spot in heaven. The irony of that discussion, on that day, after that display!

Another memorable narcissistic moment was with James and John. Well, actually, with their mother too. The mother of James and John approached Jesus, and told Him, "Grant that one of these two sons of mine may sit at your right and the other at your left in your kingdom" (Matthew 20:21). That's a bold request, isn't it? They wanted to use Jesus to gain a position of power. The way Mark records it, he remembers the brothers saying bluntly, "We want you to do for us whatever we ask" (Mark 10:35).

Do today's disciples of Jesus struggle with narcissism? Consider the current Christian climate. We still have Christians approaching Jesus in the same manner of James and John saying, "Jesus, do for me whatever I ask."

Now, "hold on" you might say. Doesn't God want us to pray and ask for things? Yes.[9] Doesn't God promise to hear all our prayers and encourage us to believe He can do it? Yes.[10] The problem is a sky-high expectation without a "thy will be done" consideration.[11] When narcissism mixes with Christianity, Jesus is merely a genie using His almighty power to make earthly life better. Some Christians even leave Jesus when He doesn't do as they say. Do you sense narcissism still running through the veins of today's disciples?

Let me bring it closer still. There are narcissistic tendencies in each one of us.

We see it at the grocery store when choosing a check-out line. We don't want the slow line. If that light above our line starts blinking, we just might lose it. Why do we want the fastest line? "It's ALL about me." We see it in an argument. It's so hard to say we're sorry. It's much easier to make excuses and point the finger. Why? "It's ALL about me." We see it on the highways. What's behind our road rage when we get cut off? "It's ALL about me." We see it on social media. What photos do we choose to post? The one that makes us look good, or the one where others look good? Do we even look at the faces of the others in the picture we posted? How many photos did it take to get the perfect shot? What's behind this? "It's ALL about me."

Spiritually speaking, narcissism is devastating.

I remember a class I took at seminary with seemingly one point. Dean Brenner's major point was to prove that we were all pre-programmed to think we could win salvation. He often referred to the "opinio legis," which means "the opinion of the law." He taught us that we all have an opinion of God's law. Our natural opinion is that we keep God's law, and He rewards us with heaven. Most people still believe this. The prevailing thought about salvation is that we can be good enough to win heaven. It's our spiritual default setting.

The premise of every religion, apart from Christianity, is this: you must be good to get to heaven. This premise preaches perfectly to the ears of the spiritual narcissist. The spiritual narcissist says, "Amen. Of course I win salvation. Of course I must be good. In fact, let me show you how good I am." Reminds me of a discussion Jesus had with a rich man. This man thought he had kept all of God's law perfectly. Until Jesus invited him to leave all his riches and follow Him.[12]

Every religion, apart from Christianity, is fueled by the rules. Every gathering in these religions, feeds the idea that heaven is won by good behavior. The inevitable by-product of these religions is hypocrisy. So religious circles are filled with hypocrites, who have to put on a good face as if they were good people, knowing they have failed at the game of rule-following some time back.

But enough about other religions. What about Christianity and Christians? We who know only Jesus can save us. "I am the way and the truth and the life. No one comes to the Father except through me" (John 14:6). We who know good people don't go to heaven, because no one is good. "For all have sinned and fall short of the glory of God" (Romans 3:23). We who know salvation is a gift of grace, and not accomplished by our works. "For it is by grace you have been saved, through faith—and this is not from yourselves, it is the gift of God—not by works, so that no one can boast." (Ephesians 2:8-9). We who know God rescued us when we could not save ourselves? "But God demonstrates his own love for us in this: While we were still sinners, Christ died for us" (Romans 5:8). Are we better off? Can we avoid the narcissistic tendencies of others?

When you think about it, every sin is spiritual narcissism. Every sin comes from a self-centered heart who in a moment of exaggerated self-importance is telling God, "My way is better than Your way, my needs are more important than Your glory, and my feelings trump Your feelings about it." The sins people think are big, like murder and sleeping around. To the sins people think are little, like lying and gossiping, being greedy and discontent. At its core, every sin speaks the same line to God which is, "it's ALL about me."

Do you see the problem now? Even if you rolled your eyes at the beginning, did some truth reach out and grab you? Did you start to sense narcissistic tendencies even in you? And where can this lead if it's not addressed, if it's not attacked, if it's not changed by the power of the Holy Spirit...

"It's ALL about me" leads to a meaningless life.

Can you imagine a world where your wildest dreams come true? Where everything on the vision board is checked off, and in the order you hoped it would happen? What would it feel like? What would you say about life then?

I can tell you with certainty. There was a man who attained the wildest of earthly dreams. Everything people chase after today - money, fame, romance, and success - was his times a thousand. He was so rich that in his day silver was common. He was so famous that other famous people would travel far distances just to have an audience with him. He was so successful that an ancient wonder of the world was built by his hands. He was such a heart throb, that he had over a thousand lovers.

This was Solomon. You can read about him in the Bible. It's a great story about a young boy who asked for wisdom, and God gave him that - and the world. But as he got wrapped up into the world and away from God, he lost what truly mattered. He wrote a book about it called Ecclesiastes. Some say it was his memoir looking back at life. Yet, out of all he experienced, gained, and accomplished, he says they were meaningless apart from God. Here are his words:

> "I undertook great projects: I built houses for myself and planted vineyards...I amassed silver and gold for myself, and the treasure of

kings and provinces. I acquired male and female singers, and a harem as well—the delights of a man's heart. I became greater by far than anyone in Jerusalem before me. I denied myself nothing my eyes desired; I refused my heart no pleasure…Yet when I surveyed all that my hands had done and what I had toiled to achieve, **everything was meaningless**, a chasing after the wind; nothing was gained under the sun" (Ecclesiastes 2:4, 8-11).

But it's not just a renowned Christian who said this. Many have come to the conclusion that when "it's ALL about me," life is meaningless. It's Tom Brady, who after winning Super Bowls said, "Why do I have those Super Bowl rings and still think there's something out there greater. There's got to be more than this."[13] It's Jim Carrey who arrived as an actor and Hollywood elite who said, "I wish everyone could get rich and famous and everything they ever dreamed of so they can see that that's not the answer."[14]

And so if what we do from here is make life about ourselves… if we only pursue the better house, better vacation, and better job…if we're only about more money, and more success…if we're laser focused about making life the best for us, and using God to help us do it…then we might also wind up with a memoir that could be titled, "My life was meaningless."

Unless there is a better way. At this point I don't mean to over-sell the answer of the book, but here goes anyway. The answer in this book could keep you from a wasted life. The answer in this book could create instant impact for the good in every arena of life. This is the answer that your friends hope to see in you, what your kids need of you, and what gives God the greatest glory.

The Christian answer to an age of narcissism is: "It's NOT about me."

And you know who gave us this answer? Jesus. And He knows a thing or two about how this life should be lived.

Do you remember the account with James and John - when they asked Him for whatever they wanted? Jesus didn't leave that occasion without a lesson. As the disciples argued over their request to have the highest seats in heaven, Jesus entered in. He told them what the people of this world do with power. They live as if it were all about them, and use and abuse other people. And then Jesus said, "Not so with you. Instead, whoever wants to become great among you must be your servant, and whoever wants to be first must be slave of all. For even the Son of Man did not come to be served, but to serve, and to give his life as a ransom for many" (Mark 10:43-45).

"It's not about me." It's not only the teaching given to the disciples. It's behind what led the Son of God to save the world. And it's the answer that changes everything. It's the answer behind the most important principles in a Christian's life. It's the answer that if lived by, will create the greatest impact with the mere moments we have on earth.

So let's see how. But first, a deep dive into the life of the One who lived it. Let's talk about Jesus.

STUDY QUESTIONS

1) Have you ever believed the world revolves around you? What experience do you have with narcissism? Who stands out as a notable narcissist to you?

2) Read John 13:1-17 and Luke 22:24-30. What strikes you about these accounts from Maundy Thursday? Do you think the disciples of Jesus were narcissists? Why or why not?

3) What areas of life have you seen a proclivity to put yourself first - driving, selfies, or grocery lines? Any other examples?

4) In what ways is Christianity different than other religions? Read Romans 3:21-28. How does salvation through good works feed our narcissist tendencies?

5) What activities have you found to be meaningless? What have you found true meaning in? What comes to your mind when you think of areas that we need to declare, "it's not about me"?

THE SOLUTION

Christmas is NOT the most wonderful time of the year.

Before you call me Scrooge, bear with me. The problem is not the music, the lights, or the food. The music is great, and I blare Trans-Siberian Orchestra and Mariah Carey with the best of them. The lights - I love the lights! Each neighbor trying to outdo each other chasing after Clark Griswold's model home. And the food is something else. Growing up, my grandmother would bring tiger meat, clam chowder, and herring. Oh the smells! By the way, tiger meat isn't actually from tigers, as I learned much later on. It is raw ground beef you spread on rye bread topped with onions and black pepper.

Then there's Santa. I won't go too far with this one, but I took great joy when my six-year-old daughter tried to convert Santa. She left a note asking if Santa knew Jesus. That was pretty epic in my mind. Jesus over Santa, can I get an amen!?

Part of the struggle with Christmas is that it's pregnant with expectation, but it never delivers. We expect it to be magical, to live up to our childhood dreams, and that one perfect Christmas. And then we grow older and it never does. People leave. The kids grow up, and soon they will be hosting their own Christmas celebrations. Hearts are heavy because of those who can no longer be with us. We miss grandparents and others who died around Christmastime. For those who can get together, it's complicated navigating imperfect families. Beyond that, our busy lives are made busier with Christmas shopping, Christmas cards, Christmas parties and pageants. We may expect a big gift that no one can give like a Lexus with a big bow on it. Because of this, it's not just Elvis who experiences a "Blue Christmas." Many people struggle with heavy emotions and depression during Christmas.

But that still is not the main reason Christmas isn't the most wonderful time of the year. The struggle has to do with Jesus.

Jesus is the reason for the season. And the message of Christmas is beautiful *for us*. After five hundred years without a word from God since the time of the prophet Malachi, God enters in with His messengers, the angels. And the message of the angels at Christmas is beyond good! "Glory to God in the highest heaven, and on earth peace to those on whom his favor rests" (Luke 2:14). Because Jesus came, we have peace with a holy God! Hallelujah! Jesus is proof that God kept His promises, and did not give up on us! Jesus is the "offspring of the woman" promised from the very beginning, who will reverse the curse of sin, and crush the devil's head.[1] Our Hero, Jesus, is here! Jesus has come to save us! Yes, the message of Christmas is indeed beautiful *for us*!

But have you ever considered Christmas from Jesus' point of view? How beautiful, how magical is Christmas *for Him*?

The Almighty Creator is allowing Himself to be cared for by the imperfect creation. God is being nursed and changed - how humbling! The One who reigned supreme over all things is born into a peasant's family. The

King of kings doesn't line up a five-star hotel for Himself, but allows Himself to be born in a barn. No fine linens and luxurious touches - just the stench of animals and the scratch of hay in a manger. The family He lived with fled to Egypt, because from the very first day of His life this world has a seething, unquenchable hate for Him.

And we have the audacity at Christmas to give off the impression to Jesus, "Welcome! Isn't it great here?! Don't you just love what we've done with the place?!" We dress up our nativity scenes with beautiful snowfall. We sing songs that set the mood for splendor and wonder. We sing about calm and bright and everything right. Yet, this world is the sandcastle sin smashed. Christmas is when Jesus took on flesh to observe the mess. And we, with our narcissistic tendencies, forget that while the Christmas story is beautiful *for us* - it is one of the most difficult, painful, and cruel experiences *for Him*.

Jesus coming to earth shouldn't be compared to a loved one visiting our place from a foreign land. As if the goal of Christmas was to show Him the beautiful sights, and our favorite spots. No way! Jesus coming to earth is like the D-Day invasion of Normandy Beach. He sits alone in the U-boat with no one to comfort Him, ready for the door to be let down and the battle to begin. And make no mistake, Christmas means war for Jesus. Almost everyone either misunderstands Him, wants to manipulate Him, or hates Him. He is about to bear every pain imaginable for us until…He dies. But again, "Welcome!"

Consider it this way. It's very easy to get used to the finer things. This last summer our family rented a brand new Ford Explorer. It was amazing! The interior was immaculate with smooth-as-butter leather seats. The technology and interior screen was state of the art, syncing seamlessly with my phone and Apple CarPlay. The handling was incredibly responsive, as we pulled off one of many U-turns driving in a new place. And the Blumer family had a ball feeling like first class in that brand new car.

When we stepped back into our 2008 Prius with 230,000 miles it felt like a demotion. Everything was worse, uncomfortable, and ugly.

Have you ever been downgraded? You went from a big house to a smaller house? You went from 5-star service on a vacation to demanding rudeness from co-workers and clients when you got back home?

Now we are starting to see the Christmas story through Jesus' lens. He goes from all the angels' adoration in heaven, to hate on earth. He goes from all-powerful Ruler and Coordinator of history, to a tiny baby without the power to feed Himself. Christmas is Jesus' ultimate demotion.

But Christmas proves Jesus operated with one simple premise here on earth: "It's not about me." If it had to be all about Him, He would have never come. But because it wasn't, He left the glory of heaven for the pain of earth.

Consider what Paul wrote concerning this in his letter to the Christians in Philippi,

> "Who, being in very nature God, did not consider equality with God something to be used to his own advantage; rather, he made himself nothing by taking the very nature of a servant, being made in human likeness. And being found in appearance as a man, he humbled himself by becoming obedient to death—even death on a cross" (Philippians 2:6-8).

Christmas is simply a microcosm of His time on earth. From conception to crib to cross to crypt is a period of time referred to by theologians as His "humiliation." And when considering Jesus' humiliation, the best explanation is that He set aside His power. He did what Paul is referring to when he said, "He (Jesus) did not consider equality with God something to be used to his own advantage" (Philippians 2:6). Basically, Jesus didn't make even the fullness of the Godhead about Him! He set aside his Godly activity and power and rights. And we see this humility throughout Jesus' earthly life, not just at Christmas.

If we take Jesus' lens, on what day did He wake up saying, "It's all about me today. I'm going to get what I deserve, and take what I want." On what day did the Father tell Him, "You do you, boo." It's laughable.

Imagine if when tempted by the Devil, Jesus lived like it were all about Him. Now, the Devil is a dog on God's leash and has no power but what afforded him by God. So Jesus wouldn't have had to fast for forty days. He wouldn't have had to go through the agony and burning of those temptations. If it was all about Jesus that day, one of two things would have happened. He would either bow down to Satan to avoid the cross and retain some power. More likely, He would have sealed Satan's fate at that moment for daring to mess with Him. Jesus would have made him like the other demons locked in gloomy dungeons immediately.

But Jesus wasn't in that moment for Himself.

Imagine if before Herod, Jesus lived as if it were all about Him. As Herod invites Him to do miracles, and to put on a performance like some circus clown, what if Jesus made Herod juggle? Or what if Jesus opened Herod's eyes to the end of time, where Jesus is reigning visibly above all things.

What if He showed the surpassing power and glory of that kingdom, and Herod bending the knee.

But Jesus didn't stand before Herod because it was all about Him.

Imagine if on the cross Jesus lived as if it were all about Him. How I would have loved if He silenced the scoffers. When they taunt Him saying, "He saved others…but he can't save himself" (Matthew 27:42). Oh, if only He took His power back in that moment and turned them into rats, or zapped them dead! If only the ground opened to swallow them in that moment, or if they died of dysentery! What sweet justice that would have been!

But Jesus wasn't on the cross for Himself.

Jesus lived and taught, "it's not about me" perhaps, most memorably the day before He died.

There they were waiting for the meal. And Jesus chose the lowest job possible. In a day when the greatest form of travel was on foot, He decided to wash His disciple's feet. We don't know what condition those feet were in, or what they stepped in before they came to supper. What we do know is what Jesus was trying to model. He was trying to show them by example how life should be lived. For others. To serve them. To wash each other's feet - figuratively. To be willing to do the hardest, dirtiest, and most thankless work for the sake of someone else.

When He was done washing their feet He said, "Now that I, your Lord and Teacher, have washed your feet, you also should wash one another's feet. I have set you an example that you should do as I have done for you" (John 13:14-15).

But now the big question. Why? Why would Jesus do this? Why wouldn't He live for Himself, though He out of all people had the right to do so? Let me explain.

In Chicago there is a store called, "American Girl." At this store you can buy very expensive dolls that wear expensive clothing. You can bring these dolls to the store to get their hair done at the salon. There is a restaurant where you can eat with your doll, and they have a special chair for your doll to sit in. There is a target audience for this experience, and an adult male is not the target. Walking in as a man the employees kindly show empathy. Their eyes communicate, "We know this isn't fun for you, but if you're lucky it will all be over soon."

A few years back my wife and I took our girls to get an American Girl Doll. We spent a lot of money, and I endured an experience that was not designed for me. Why? Love does crazy things, doesn't it? Love gives. Love endures. Love goes beyond all reasonable measure. Love wants to wow someone by its very expression. And we love our girls, so yes, I went to "American Girl."

Back to Jesus. Here's His why: Love. Crazy love. Amazing love. Unfailing love. A love that gives beyond all reasonable measure. A love that endures. A love that surpasses our understanding of earthly love. A love designed to wow us.

This is what you have in Jesus. This is what makes Him the only lasting treasure in a world of transitory pleasures and fake goods. He loves you and has proved that love. The temptation He endured by the Devil was for you. It was Him passing temptation's test for you, to win for you righteousness. He was tempted in every way but was found without sin.[2]

He stood before Herod for you. He would set aside His power and glory in that moment to work His way to the cross. Because the cross was for you. It means that any sin you have done, any sin you are currently struggle with, any sin you might do in the future - it's forgiven. The payment He made on the cross covers that sin.[3]

If you're new to the message of Christianity, or If It's been a while. This message is what is so different than any other religion or message. Salvation is not contingent on your performance, because it was contingent the performance of Jesus.[4] His love isn't yours because you were better and brighter than most. The only answer for why He loves you is this: He loves you because He chose to love you. He loved you when you had nothing to give Him. He loved you at your worst.[5] And He still loves you.

And do you know what this love means? This love means you will never be alone, because He will never leave you.[6] This love means as long as you are on earth He will be working on your behalf.[7] Even the horrible things that happen He promises to redeem because He loves you. It means you will always have enough.[8] You will have enough health, food, provision until the day when He'd rather see you face to face. This love means you don't need to find your security in the fleeting, failing love of others. Others, who even at their best can't give close to what Jesus gave, and at their worst simply manipulate you for their own means in the name of love. This love culminates in an eternity where we get to return to the original plan of God. The plan where pain, sadness, and death is eliminated.[9] Where we walk and talk with God and finally understand the full lengths of God's love.[10]

See the reality in Jesus is this: He made his whole life about loving and redeeming you. I consider what John said about this work, "Jesus knew that the hour had come for him to leave this world and go to the Father. Having loved his own who were in the world, he loved them to the end" (John 13:1). His whole life was a labor of love for us. "It's not about me" is what led Him to the cross, and led Him to save us.

"It's not about me" is the principle behind the salvation of the world.

Even Hollywood has picked up on the power of it. If you're like me, you have enjoyed the comic book movies, from Iron Man to Spider Man and everywhere in between. And the culmination of the Marvel movies has to be "Avengers: Endgame" when Iron Man finally has the infinity stones on his fist. He could use this power for his own benefit and live for himself. Or with the snap of his fingers he could restore the world and the many lives that Thanos took. What should he do? Spoiler alert - he snaps his fingers to save the world...but it cost him his life. One of the greatest cinematic moments highlighting the nobility of living a life that declares, "it's not about me." I could give you more, and point to culminating scenes in blockbusters like "Braveheart," "The Green Mile," and "Armageddon." Hollywood making a buck from principles Jesus taught? It wouldn't be the first time.

Do you see why I called Jesus' love a treasure? There's nothing that even comes close to it. If you lose everything else and everyone else but have Him - you still have all you need![11] **Because He is the one who made it ALL about you**, and He won't stop now. He'll give you the love, the help, the strength, and the provision needed.

Which leads me to the other why. You might have asked, "Why should I live a life that's not about me? Especially today, when no one else is?"

Well, we cannot save ourselves or add to the salvation He alone secured.[12] But what we can do with our response and daily living is proclaim with our actions, "I love you too. Thank you for loving me."[13]

Consider what Paul said about our lives responding to the love of God, "I have been crucified with Christ and I no longer live, but Christ lives in me. The life I now live in the body, I live by faith in the Son of God, who loved me and gave himself for me" (Galatians 2:20).

Jesus set us free from the reckless, fruitless, painful pursuit of ourselves.[14] He set us free from a life of meaningless ventures. He brought to us nobility, and true purpose.[15]

So are you ready to take the leap? Are you willing to trust God by living a life that's radically different? Will you declare with your life, "God I love you, and nothing else comes close!"

Let's talk about what that might look like.

STUDY QUESTIONS

1) On a scale of 1-10 how much do you like Christmas? Why? What about Christmas from Christ's lens strikes you?

2) What did Jesus give up in coming to earth? If you had almighty power, what would you do with it? If you were Jesus, when might you have been tempted to take your power back?

3) If Jesus had lived only for Himself, what would that mean for you? Because he didn't live for Himself, what does that mean for you?

4) Think on a time when you endured an experience for the sake of someone else. Why is this so hard to do?

5) What do you appreciate the most about God's love for you? Go to the "Notes" section in the back of the book for this chapter, and look up the passages. What passage is your favorite describing the activity and goodness of God?

6) List various ways you can express your love for God.

POWER

Michael Jordan has my vote for being the G.O.A.T (Greatest Of All Time). He was the king of clutch. I never had more confidence in a team than I had in the 90s Chicago Bulls with Michael Jordan. But it wasn't just that he won six championships - he did so much else. He won the slam dunk contest with a dunk often attempted but never quite reduplicated. He soared from the free throw line to the rim and consequently was dubbed "Air Jordan." In the Olympics he led USA's original Dream Team to gold, making every other country along the way look like the freshman squad was up against varsity. He even starred in "Space Jam," and defeated an alien basketball team with the help of Bugs Bunny! What couldn't Michael Jordan do?

In the 90s, Gatorade wrote a jingle about Jordan that went, "Sometimes I dream that he is me. You've got to see that's how I dream to be. I dream I move, I dream I groove. Like Mike if I could be like Mike." And I sang along, "I wanna be, wanna be, wanna be like Mike."[1] I, along with every other kid my age, wanted to be like Mike.

Until…his Hall of Fame induction speech. I'm not sure I've seen a grown man crying more - the waterworks were unbelievable. There was my childhood hero getting his well-deserved recognition and rightful place.

But Michael Jordan's tears were not endearing. He was crying not so much because he was touched by all the people who wished him well and celebrated him. He was crying because he had an axe to grind against any naysayer. To him this was a defining moment over anyone who ever doubted him. He talked about his competitive fire and those who put "logs of wood" on that fire.[2] He talked about his varsity coach picking another player over him, and how he was going to prove the coach made a huge mistake. He referenced Buzz Peterson, who was named Player of the Year, and Jordan didn't believe he deserved it because he hadn't played him yet. Story after story was the same, proving how he showed them all.

"The Last Dance" documentary picked up on this similar theme. From punching Steve Kerr to perhaps blacklisting Isiah Thomas from the Dream Team - for Michael Jordan it was all about him. His power was his competitive nature, and so he took the credit.

Contrast that with some achievements in the Bible. Let's consider just three.

David vs. Goliath. Here we have a sixteen-year-old shepherd boy versus a seasoned warrior, and the champion of a nation. Goliath is over nine feet tall with a spear tip weighing fifteen pounds and armor weighing almost one hundred pounds.[3] He is battle tested and battle ready. No wonder Goliath laughs at David and calls him a dog. From a human standpoint, the competition is not even close.

But David has something Goliath does not - God on his side. And David's confidence to enter the fight is not about who he is. Though he references his time fighting a bear and a lion, his confidence comes from a different place. He approaches Goliath and says, "You come against me with sword and spear and javelin, but **I come against you in the name of the Lord**

Almighty, the God of the armies of Israel, whom you have defied" (1 Samuel 17:45). And with God on his side, he defeated Goliath and cut off his head. *The greatest one-on-one fight was won because of the power of the Lord.*

Gideon's 300 vs. 135,000 Midianites. Have you heard of the Battle of Thermopylae? In this battle 300 Greek soldiers from Sparta were left to fight innumerable Persians. It's a story of their bravery, as they kept fighting when the odds were not in their favor.[4] Unfortunately, they died and lost the Battle of Thermopylae.

Did you know the Bible records a similar true story between the Israelites and the Midianites? The number of Midianites is described this way, "The Midianites, the Amalekites and all the other eastern peoples had settled in the valley, thick as locusts. Their camels could no more be counted than the sand on the seashore" (Judges 7:12).

And what did Gideon have? Courage? No, he needed convincing. Many soldiers? No, his Israelite forces were whittled down from 32,000 to 10,000 to 300. Flawless character? If you think so, I encourage you to read the end of the story and learn about Gideon's ephod.[5] So what did Gideon have? God on his side. As he goes out with the 300 they shout, "**A sword for the Lord** and for Gideon" (Judges 7:20). ("For Gideon" reminds us how the power of God is still at work in the severely flawed). And because God fought for them and terrified the enemy, 300 Israelites defeated 135,000 Midianites! Let me help you appreciate the scale of this. It would be as if the citizens of the United States went to war with Fiji in hand-to-hand combat, and Fiji won. *So the greatest underdog battle in history was won because of the power of the Lord.*

Elijah vs. 850 false prophets. This has to be one of my favorite displays of the glory of God. Basically, it's a dual between God and so-called gods. The prophets of Baal and Elijah set up altars and ask for fire from heaven to burn up an animal offering. The prophets of Baal go first, and they are praying, dancing, and cutting themselves. But nothing happens. Because of this, Elijah taunts them and says, "Shout louder! Surely he is a god! Perhaps he is deep in thought, or busy, or traveling. Maybe he is sleeping and must be awakened" (1 Kings 18:27). That's spiritual trash talking at its finest, yet not for the sake of Elijah but for the renown of God.

Then it's Elijah's turn. And he drenches the offering with water, knowing things that are wet don't burn well. He calls on God saying, "Answer me, Lord, answer me, so these people will know that **you, Lord, are God**" (1 Kings 18:37). The Lord answers, sending a fire that not only burns the offering and water that had drenched it, but the fire burns down the stone altar! (I've never seen stones burn up, usually, stones line a fire pit because they don't burn up!) *And the greatest spiritual dual was won because of the power of the Lord.*

Do you see the crazy, incredible power of God? It's the power that spoke a word and spotted the sky with stars. It's the power that split the Red Sea with wind that He spun up. It's the power that crafted every creature, clothed every flower, and cultivated every plant. It's the power of Jesus that gave sight to the blind, made a cripple walk again, and raised the dead. There is no power like the power of God!

What's my point in all of this? Because we are all pre-programmed to believe "it's all about me," we could believe in our power and the glory is ours. **When we accept "it's not about me," we rely on the power of God and the glory is His.**

See, it's not just Michael Jordan who is tempted to rely on his strength and receive his glory. It's our whole culture where it's common to say, "I've never been given a handout." "I have to pull myself up by my own bootstraps." "I have this because I put in the hard work," or, "I've earned it." This has always been the way of people, so Scripture is riddled with warnings against this mentality.

I love the Psalm that says, "His pleasure is not in the strength of the horse, nor his delight in the legs of the warrior; the Lord delights in those who fear him, who put their hope in his unfailing love" (Psalm 147:10-11).

I consider the Scripture when the Israelites had just taken over the Promised Land. He warned them, "You may say to yourself, 'My power and the strength of my hands have produced this wealth for me.' But **remember the Lord your God, for it is he who gives you the ability to produce wealth**, and so confirms his covenant, which he swore to your ancestors, as it is today" (Deuteronomy 8:17).

How do we get there? How do we remember we need the Lord's power and continue to rely on it? What might prompt us to give Him the praise when we have the platform? Let's dive in.

Incredibly, Roe v. Wade was overturned in the Supreme Court.[6] What a watershed moment for our country! I honestly did not believe this would ever happen, and it's been the center of political debates for decades. While there are cases when you might have to consider mom's health versus the baby's health - in general this is such great news that protects life! But I believe it's such great news because here is what we know. God had us in mind before our parents had us in mind. God worked in the womb of our mothers to ensure we would be here.

Look at the words of this beautiful Psalm, "Your eyes saw my unformed body; all the days ordained for me were written in your book before one of them came to be. For you created my inmost being; **you knit me together** in my mother's womb. I praise you because I am fearfully and wonderfully made" (Psalm 139:16, 13-14).

To put it another way, who chose your birthday? Did you raise your hand and tell God, "Hey, I'd like to be born on April 4th. Oh yeah, and while you're knitting me together, I have a few requests. If I could be really good at basketball with the ability to dunk, that'd be great. Do you think You could knit green eyes and blonde hair as You're working? Could I also be born in the United States, not Russia? Could I have two really awesome, stable parents who happen to love You? And one last thing, could You give me a sense of humor, that'd be awesome, and please not the cheesy type."

Did you have that moment with God telling Him your birthday and your laundry list of desires? Me neither.

This truth reminds me of what I've memorized and recited many times along the way as a Wisconsin Evangelical Lutheran Synod (WELS) Lutheran. Martin Luther, in explaining how God the Father is the Creator wrote, "I believe that God made me and every creature and that he gave me my body and soul, eyes, ears and all my members, my mind and all my abilities."[7] God chose me, before I could choose me. God doled out gifts before I knew what to ask for, or what skills I'd like to have.

If it's been a while since you've thought about that, you're not alone. We forget...a lot. So what does God use so we don't forget? How could He work in our lives so that we are in constant appreciation of His power?

Let me ask, have you ever been stuck? Are you stuck in a situation right now? Let me tell you of a time when I was stuck in a pretty bad situation. It was way beyond what my power could do.

I'm a bit of a car guy, which is why I own a Toyota Prius.[8] (Ha, God's got my Porsche waiting in heaven for me). And because I'm a car guy, I find myself working on cars. (Truth: that actually has less to do with me being a car guy, and more to do with me being a cheap guy). On one occasion, I was going to fix the fuel neck on my minivan. I had to do this because while filling up at a gas station, a stranger kindly pointed out the gas was not going into my car, but leaking all over the ground next to my car. That was embarrassing. The fuel neck had rusted through and caused the leak. So with the power of Youtube and my can-do attitude, I got the part and went to work. I took out the old fuel neck, which was so rusted it disintegrated in my hands as I was taking it off. I tried to put the new fuel neck on and…it didn't fit. It was the right part for the right place, but I had no idea how to get it on. I was stuck. Youtube had no more advice to offer, and I had no more strength or ideas. So what did I have to do?

I called for help. Thankfully, I have a good friend who is a mechanic. Brian to the rescue! And what had me stuck for two hours took him two minutes to diagnose and figure out. He had to bend the fuel neck into place, and he used the jack stand to do it because he's amazing. And I realized some problems we just can't solve on our own. We need help.

So what I find is this… **God's remedy for our "it's all about me" mentality is to allow us to get stuck.** He gives us kids, and then we run up against situations where we don't know what to do. What do you do with a colicky baby? He allows us to feel the financial pinch at times, and we don't see how it's going to work out. How will there be enough? He allows overwhelming circumstances where the strength and ideas we have are far too few. How will I get through this? (Have you believed the Christian lie that God wouldn't give you more than you can handle?[9] Truth: He does it all the time). And why?

So we call Him for help.

I don't give nicknames to many psalms, but I gave one to Psalm 121. I call it the "Worry Crusher." It's a psalm I gave to my daughter Nadia when she was having night terrors. It's a psalm I try to repeat over in my mind before bed. It's a psalm I assign to others as homework and ask them to count how many times it says the Lord is watching over you. (Five times by the way).

But it starts with these powerful words, "I lift up my eyes to the mountains—where does my help come from" (Psalm 121:1). This is a psalm dedicated to those who would travel up to the temple in Jerusalem for worship. Travel back in the day was treacherous. Beautiful, I'm sure with mountains and vistas, but treacherous. Robbers could hide behind those mountains to attack. You were exposed to the extremes of nature. I'm sure the writer of Psalm 121 would have been a car guy if that were an option for his travel. Because he didn't have a car, he needed help. And he tells us where his help comes from.

"My help comes from the Lord, **the Maker of heaven and earth**" (Psalm 121:2). What a great description! The One who is our Helper also happened to make heaven and earth! It seems whenever God defends His power and authority as God, He refers to creation.[10] And that means that our Helper has an arm that is not too short to help us in any and every situation.[11]

And help He does.

Consider Alcoholics Anonymous. It is one of the most successful groups that combats addictions. Most are familiar with the opening line, "Hi, my name is _____, and I'm an alcoholic." And you might know there is a twelve step program. The first of those steps? "We admitted we were powerless over alcohol." The second? "Came to believe that a Power greater than ourselves could restore us to sanity."[12] It is that Power that has released so many from this harmful addiction.

We know who that Power is. The Lord, the Maker of heaven and earth.

So here's the opportunity. You know that area where you are stuck right now? Out of love I need to tell you, you are not enough. You do not have enough strength or insight or power to handle it. But God does. His power is always enough. I encourage you to invite His power into your situation regularly. For the big things, like when your loved one is battling cancer. For the small things, like when you have to take a test or are going for a job interview. **When we choose to live declaring "it's not about me," we have the opportunity to tap into an unlimited power source.**

Consider the essence of salvation. It's the idea that we were stuck! And our attempts to get unstuck made us more stuck still! The good we needed to do, we didn't do. The evil we don't want to do, we've done. That's what Paul said even after conversion.[13] And it didn't matter how much we tried. Like truck tires stuck in mud that keep spinning, so our attempts to be good enough drove us deeper into being stuck.

Until Jesus. Until the grace of God. Until the power of the Almighty unleashed on our behalf. And Jesus does for us what we cannot do for ourselves. Jesus displayed His power over the law, as He was tempted in every way but was found without sin.[14] Jesus displayed His power over our sin, as He paid the punishment for our sins in full on the cross.[15] Best yet, Jesus displayed His power over this world of brokenness and the most broken part of it - death - by rising from the dead![16] We are saved, set free, unstuck by the power of God, and it is the only power that works for salvation.[17]

Consider the beauty of this truth through these words, "As for you, you were dead in your transgressions and sins (*you can't get more stuck than that!*)...But because of his great love for us, God, who is rich in mercy, made us alive (*His power*) with Christ even when we were dead in transgressions—it is by grace you have been saved" (Ephesians 2:1, 4-5).

So where do we go from here? How can this understanding drive our vision for the future?

One of my favorite pictures of a Christian comes from a movie set. When filming a movie, lighting is extremely important. Because of this, there are set workers whose only job is to hold a light reflector. When light comes their way, they direct the light onto the shot. They are not the focal point. Their job is to let everyone know what the focal point is.

That's the Christian life in a nutshell. We're simply holding a light reflector. When light comes our way...when attention comes our way...when applause comes our way...when accolades come our way...we point all of that to the One who deserves it - our Savior, Jesus.

Someone who exhibited this understanding in an incredible way is Monty Williams. Monty Williams is not a pastor, but he gave one of the best sermons I've ever heard. Monty Williams is the head coach for the Phoenix Suns. In 2016 his wife was tragically killed in a car accident. A lot of attention came his way, and he knew exactly what to do with it. The eulogy he gave for his wife directed that attention onto the one name that matters for all time - Jesus. Here are just a couple of lines from his speech,

> *"We can't lose sight of the fact that God loves us and that's what my wife and that's what I, however badly, exhibit on a daily basis....But God does love us. God will work this out. My wife is in heaven. God loves us. God is love. And when we walk away from this place today, let's celebrate because my wife is where we all need to be. And I'm envious of that....Let's not lose sight of what's important. God is important. What Christ did on the cross is important."*[18]

That's an incredible confession at an attention grabbing moment.

I remember my opportunity. I was a seminary student on a choir tour to California, when I was called up to be a contest on "The Price is Right."

The night before I was sleeping at my friend's house, and in my conversation with God while in the guest bunkbed I made a plan. If I got on the game show, I would point people to Jesus. I had it all planned out. When they asked who I wanted to say hi to before spinning the wheel I would say, "I want to thank my Lord and Savior Jesus Christ for the victory He won for all people! He is the only way to heaven." (That last part is what some have labeled a "truth grenade," but I thought it was balanced with the invitation for all to have victory. Anyway, I was younger then).

I was one of the first people picked that day. On contestants row in the first round! This was my chance. It took until the fifth round of bidding to finally win. I used God's number $777 as a bid for some commercial lawn tools and it worked! I got on stage, hugged my BFF, Drew Carey, and played Bullseye. I won again! I picked two small bottles of light olive oil and it hit the Bullseye with the total between ten and twelve dollars. A funky retro bedroom set with a memory foam mattress was all mine! And…here was my chance. Right before I got up to spin the wheel they told me I would not have a chance to speak. Rather, they were going to pan to the crowd where the Wisconsin Lutheran Seminary Chorus was and they were going to sing. I thought, "Of course God, they have plenty of songs to give You glory, and '**it's not about me**.'" So they pan to the crowd and…they sing a song in German that's not about Jesus.

Ugh. I failed. I felt like I didn't live up to my end of the deal. So the next day reflecting on everything, I made a commitment. I'll just spend the rest of my life telling people about Jesus.

What moments did you succeed in giving the glory to Jesus? What moments passed you by? What would it look like for all the attention and glory you receive to be reflected back to Jesus?

As we close this chapter, there is this helpful practice among my brother pastors. Whenever someone is done presenting a paper or talk that took a great deal of work, they put the letters "SDG" on the final page.

Know what it stands for? It's Latin, and it stands for *Soli Deo Gloria*. Which when translated is "To God alone be the glory." I like that phrase. I'm hoping you do too. When people see us, they miss the point. When people see Jesus, they have everything they need to be wowed forever.

STUDY QUESTIONS

1) What sticks out to you as evidence for God's power? Where have you experienced God's strength in your own life?

2) What is one of your greatest talents? Read Psalm 139:13-16. Who gave you your gifts, abilities, and opportunities? How can you give God glory by using your talents?

3) Think on a season you were stuck in a bad situation. How did God make a way?

4) Read Ephesians 2:1-10. How did God bring you to salvation according to those verses? According to v.10, why did God make you the way you are?

5) Has there ever been a spotlight moment where you could give God the glory? In what ways can you put more attention on God and His glory right now?

Caveat: This chapter is written from a Christian man's point of view. The experience of sex has some very unique differences based on gender. My attempt in this chapter is to speak to both men and women, and to hold women in the highest regard as co-equals and co-heirs, and daughters of the most high God.

However, I did not attempt to represent a women's point of view with the humble admission that as a man I did not think I could speak authentically to that experience. I did not want dishonor that experience claiming to understand what I do not.

SEX

The power of sex can **destroy** the strongest men.

Bill Cosby held sway over our society for decades. I will never forget sitting in our family room as my dad played the record of "Bill Cosby: Himself." I still remember busting a gut on the brown shag carpet in our home in Beaver Dam. I liked it so much that I subjected my friends, a whole bus of band members, and anyone who would give me some time to listen to it. For a while I had most of his bit on chocolate cake memorized. "EGGS, EGGS are in chocolate cake. And milk - oh goodie! And wheat, that's nutrition!!"[1] Sunday nights were family time, and like many who grew up in the 80s we gathered around to watch "The Cosby Show." Dr. Heathcliff Huxtable was America's Dad. The character he portrayed was rather hard not to like, if not love. Dr. Huxtable won hearts with the goofy looks he would give his children, the dancing his family did on the stairs of their house, and the overall wise counsel he gave. He was esteemed so much that he wrote a best-selling book entitled, "Fatherhood." This is a man who said about parenting, "In spite of the six thousand manuals on child raising in the bookstores, child raising is still a dark continent and no one really knows anything. You just need a lot of love and luck - and, of course, courage."[2] That's proof positive that he knows a thing or two about the nature of kids.

Yet Bill Cosby's name is so marred in our society today, you may have had a hard time reminiscing, even if you had similar fond memories. Countless women have come out against him claiming sexual misconduct of some sort. In 2018, Bill Cosby was found guilty on three counts of felony aggravated indecent assault. This came from the accusations of Andrea Constand, an employee at his alma mater, Temple University.[3] In 2021, the Supreme Court overturned the ruling citing a "process violation" by the prosecution.[4] In 2022, a case involving Judy Huth was settled for $500,000 with the accusation that in 1975 she was sexually abused.[5]

But it isn't just strong celebrities, it's strong men of God that have been destroyed by the power of sex. Consider Ravi Zacharias. Ravi was a powerful preacher with wise words like, "Jesus did not come into this world to make bad people good. He came to make dead people live."[6] He wrote over thirty books, hosted radio talks shows, and Ravi Zacharias International Ministries touched many, many lives. He was admired for being a faithful man of God committed to the truth.

After his death in 2020, there have been numerous charges against him. He was charged with sexual abuse stemming from massage parlors that he owned. He was accused of giving financial aid to needy women in exchange for sexual favors. He has countless women crying out against him from many different countries.[7]

But this is nothing new. The power of sex destroyed the Bible's strongest man.

Sampson was God's chosen judge to deliver the Israelites from the Philistines. He was given superhuman strength from God. Sampson was a real life superhero who tore apart a lion with his bare hands, who killed a thousand men with a donkey's jawbone, and who pushed down a temple that held thousands.[8]

And Sampson was told by God how to guard his strength. He was to maintain the vow of the Nazarite. It was a three-part vow that included 1) not being around dead bodies, 2) not drinking wine, and 3) not cutting his hair. Sampson danced around God's directive his entire life.[9] But his dance came to a deadly end because of Delilah.

Now I'll be honest. It's implied that sex led to Sampson's downfall, but it's not an illogical stretch to make this implication. Sampson was known for promiscuity.[10] He fell in love with a woman named Delilah, and spent nights sleeping at her place. The only problem with Sampson's pick is that she was a Philistine. As soon as the Philistines heard about these star-crossed lovers, they bribed Delilah to find out the secret of Sampson's strength. She took the bribe. True to form, Sampson danced around the danger with a condescending overconfidence. Delilah would ask for the secret to his strength, and he would give the wrong answer. The Philistines thought his strength was gone, and they would attack Sampson and pay the price.

But as time went by, the power of sex made Sampson stupid. Completely stupid. (Not that we can relate to this - ha). He knew the true source of his strength. He also knew that Delilah was being used to trap him. Yet the intoxicating appeal of the Sampson's favorite drug drove him to admit,"'No razor has ever been used on my head,' he said, 'because I have been a Nazarite dedicated to God from my mother's womb. If my head were shaved, my strength would leave me, and I would become as weak as any other man'" (Judges 16:17). Game, set, match. The Philistines capture him, torture and humiliate him, and it leads to his death. For what? Because Sampson wanted sex.

Ok. Did I prove the point? The power of sex can destroy the strongest men. I could go on rolling around in the mud and describing the ugliness of sexual sin, but we don't need a microscopic look at vomit to know it's gross. Can we simply admit this is heavy stuff. Sexual misconduct leads to the deepest emotions, the deepest pain, the deepest shame and regret. Sex has caused many to blush, deny, excuse, minimize, rationalize, and hide. **Sex is heavy because it is powerful, and it was made to be that way.**

So let's talk about the Creator of sex. God created sex.

You might not think about that. Your first thought might be that God is not in it, perhaps is not for it, unless you are procreating. Perhaps He doesn't want us to have fun with it. Though that is common idea, it couldn't be further from the truth.

Let's go back to the creation of sex. Ahh, the beauty of the Garden of Eden. Where perfection had its place. I imagine Adam interacting with the wildlife similar to Cinderella conducting her animal cleaners. I wonder if he walked with lions like we walk with dogs. (Cats were probably better before the fall). I imagine a constant harvest of good food to eat and from almost any tree! (We've learned farm-to-table is always best). And when the sun was shining…the birds were singing…and the flowers were in bloom…God created sex.

Well, first he created Eve. Adam was so thrilled about having a partner he erupted with the very first poem. Because Eve was crafted from Adam's rib he exclaimed, "This is now bone of my bones and flesh of my flesh; she shall be called 'woman,' for she was taken out of man" (Genesis 2:23).

I particularly like the Bible commentator who said Adam exclaimed, "Whoah man." This would be an alternate, comedic understanding for the origin of word "woman." But I think it would reflect Adam's feelings, as he was stunned by Eve's beauty. It is said that women are the fairer sex. Maybe that's because God didn't take dirt, like He did with Adam, but He took an already refined rib to make Eve? And there was unity between man and woman. The poem shows appreciation of the perfect and equal complement that God had made.

And with the butterflies still flying in the stomachs of Adam and Eve, God gave them the gift of sex. God designed a wow factor for the blessing of marriage. And with the figurative wedding bells ringing we hear, "That is why a man leaves his father and mother and is united to his wife, and **they become one flesh**. Adam and his wife were both naked, and **they felt no shame**" (Genesis 2:24).

Sex is so powerful, pastors have referred to it as glue. A glue so strong that it takes two separate people and makes them one. And that oneness was supposed to last. This reminds me of my wife's favorite part of the wedding ceremony. It's not the dress, the music, or the dancing that comes afterwards. She loves the part just after the bride and the groom have said their vows. In our circles of worship, the pastor then declares, "Those whom God has joined together, let no one separate."[11] She puts a capstone on it and whispers to me, "Boom." Mic Drop.

Think of the beauty of God's construct here. In marriage God has given a powerful uniting force meant to be used for man and woman to stick together. When they've had an argument…when the kids divide them…when they don't understand each other and feel worlds apart…glue to the rescue! And guess what - it works! I love the Hebrew word for having sex, which is literally translated "to know" someone. God had this idea that you would know your marriage partner in a way you know no one else. You would have this intimate bond that wouldn't be shared - like a secret code but so much grander. By the way, if you're ever in marriage counseling and they ask about your sex life, this is why. When you're not having sex, you're denying each other one of the most powerful forces for marital unity.

Think of the perfect reaction to marital sex. Adam and Eve had no shame. Sex wasn't dirty, bad, forbidden, or just used for procreation - it was beautiful. There were no triggers, reservations, or abuse driven by selfishness - there was simply freedom to enjoy yet another good thing from God's creation.

What did we just find? **Sex is so powerful that the only safe context for it is marriage. Sex in the context of marriage necessitates no shame.**

But does this idea make you or anyone you know bristle? How far off the mark is our society today?

In teaching the power of sex to teenagers I have a common practice. (Don't worry, it's appropriately PG). I invite them to take some Elmers glue and join two separate pieces of paper together. As we continue in conversation the glue dries. We look at the pieces of paper, and what was two has now become one. I emphasize the unity God wants between husband and wife. But then I ask what would happen if you try to separate the pieces of paper? The teens know they would get all ripped up. Part of one piece of paper would stick to the other, and vice versa. They would no longer be complete pieces of paper, but simply shreds of what used to be. Then I explain the point. This is what happens when you use the glue apart from the constant of a life-long marriage. You feel all torn-up and incomplete.

Current societal constructs when it comes to sex are destructive. Instead of teaching the boundaries and proper context of sex, the younger generation is told to experiment. Instead of teaching teens God's heart on the matter, they are taught to follow their own heart. Instead of waving the caution flag when sexual boundaries are crossed, there is celebration over the courage it took to truly express yourself.

The world we live is so far off from God's idea of sex.

I didn't grow up that way. I'm glad I didn't. Puberty is weird and hormones are real. I lived in an age where, in general, the boundaries were known, taught, and respected. But it was still a struggle wrestling with my sinful flesh. I can't imagine being told to simply express myself and listen to my heart. My sinful heart would have created a world of hurt unhinged. (More than it already has anyway). Like a kleptomaniac convinced it was ok to steal, steal I would have.

What's going on today reminds me of one of my favorite superheroes, Cyclops. Cyclops is one of the X-Men, whose superpower is the optic blast that explodes from his eyes. The optic blast is so powerful that if it is uncontrolled, it destroys anything it touches. It's the ultimate weapon. Because Cyclops doesn't want to destroy his friends or his girlfriend - he wears a visor. The visor creates control for his optic blast. Now he can use his superpower in a way that is helpful - to defeat enemies and to save the world as the X-Men do.

Our society is telling a whole generation to take the visor off when it comes to the power of sex. And the destruction is real. Let me share just three case studies. (Names have been changed for privacy).

Dillon was a gym rat. As often as I would go to LA Fitness, so often was Dillon there. Dillon was built and he knew it. He took pride flexing in the mirror. Most of us do this through glances from the corner of our eyes, but he would just stare and flex. For a while I thought this was a big part of his workout routine. I wondered, do your muscles grow when if you simply flex enough? Dillion and I became friends, and we started talking about many things. He shared that he came from California and starred in movies. He showed me clips of his cameos. He was a talented singer, and shared with me self-recordings. But Dillon was a tortured soul. What I observed casually before knowing him, was confirmed when he shared details of his past. He had an affair years ago. He referred to his actions as insanity. In his words, he had lost his mind. And for that period of pleasure he ruined the relationship he wanted the most. His agony stemmed from being divorced by his wife, and the deepest pain he dealt with was that she would not forgive him. He wanted to be forgiven, and he wanted his former life. Because neither was possible he was in agony. The power of sex destroyed his conscience.

James was a strong spiritual man who studied to be a pastor just like me. I was always impressed by how James carried himself, and by how much he knew. He like many moved on from studying to be a pastor, and I didn't hear much from him. I heard he also moved on from Christianity to a large degree, and I wondered why. Years later a confidante said it had to do with a girl. He wanted to live together with her, and he couldn't reconcile God's decrees with his desires. (I often wonder how often this is the case for losing the faith. When what I want to do is a stronger desire than living for the Lord). The power of sex destroyed his faith.

Charis was just a kid. I had a chance to learn her story through pastoral counseling. She hadn't been taught much about sex, but sex was forced upon her at a young age. One of her abusers had been abused, as is often the case. A cycle of pain continued. (Over half of women will face sexual violence of some sort).[12] Repressed memories of various forms of abuse popped up as she got older. Triggers and sexual dysfunction manifested in her marriage. Anger, illness, and various coping mechanisms were consequences. The power of sex destroyed her idea of godly sex along with so much else.

What is the answer for the mess we are in? Jesus. What a marvelous name it is! I love you Jesus.

Jesus has an answer for Dillon. Dillon needs to know and take to heart David's story. David committed adultery and murder. But David was forgiven by God. As far as the east is from the west, so far did God remove Dillon's moment of insanity from His sight. David was reconciled to the Lord and was given hope and a future. David became the primary Psalmist. David was known as a man after God's own heart,[13] even after the act. (I was able to share this with Dillon).

Jesus has an answer for James. Only Jesus has unfailing love - every other love is fleeting and failing. Running after the love of another while fleeing from His love is not the answer. Jesus is enough. He is the strength of our hearts, and our portion forever.[14]

Jesus has an answer for Charis. She is not dirty, but clean in His sight. She is worthy of love, safety, and protection, and He rescued her from the ultimate enemy. Jesus can help her reframe. She needs to know her story is represented in God's Word with Hagar. (Tamar, Rahab, and Esther too). And though Hagar was sexually mistreated she relied on the favor of the God who sees her.[15] (I was able to share this with Charis).

But what if there was a way to control the powerful gift of sex? (The power for living a holy life is always by the Holy Spirit).[16] Well, what if we approached the powerful gift of sex and declared, "it's not about me." **The remedy for the destroying power of sex is a "it's not about me" mentality.**

I think that's what Paul was advising to the Corinthian Christians. The city of Corinth in the first century had the reputation of modern-day Las Vegas. What happened in Corinth stayed in Corinth. Or maybe it didn't…to this day the standing definition of "to Corinthianize" is to be promiscuous.[17] They created a verb out of their bad reputation! Corinth was known for its widely accepted temple prostitution and brothels.

And this dysfunction bled over into the Christians gathered there. They thought the grace of God condoned sins such as a son having sexual relations with his mother.[18] There is no new sexual dysfunction under the sun.

Into this dynamic Paul wrote. And as we'll see the "it's not about me" approach to sex has three parts. **1) Respect the boundaries God created, 2) Approach marriage as an avenue for holiness, 3) Consider celibacy or periods of abstinence as a gift.**

1) Respect the boundaries God created.

> "Do you not know that your bodies are members of Christ himself? Shall I then take the **members of Christ and unite them with a prostitute**? Never! Do you not know that he who unites himself with a prostitute is **one with her in body?** For it is said, 'The two will become one flesh.' But whoever is united with the Lord is one with him in **spirit**" (1 Corinthians 6:15-17).

A common lie that compels people to go beyond God's boundaries is that sex is merely a physical act. Having sex is like playing a sport with someone. Tennis, hockey, and sex - they're all the same.

But that's not what Paul said. Paul said there's something about the nature of sex that goes beyond skin deep. It unites more than body - it unites mind, emotion, and spirit. Paul says sex is a spiritual expression. For he goes on to say,

> "Flee from sexual immorality. All other sins a person commits are outside the body, but whoever sins sexually, sins against their own body. Do you not know that **your bodies are temples of the Holy Spirit**, who is in you, whom you have received from God? You are not your own; you were bought at a price. Therefore **honor God with your bodies**" (1 Corinthians 6:18-20).

One of the more compelling cultural features of the early Christian Church is how it treated women with honor. In an age where women were viewed more like possessions than prizes, the early Christian Church provided a new norm. Jesus protected them, was friends with them, and treated them with dignity and respect.[18] This was the standard set for Christian circles. So I believe it's no wonder women wanted to be in those circles.

How well are we doing at honoring the opposite sex?

Pornography is a problem plaguing us, and stripping honor from the opposite sex. When I was growing up you in order to see porn you had to ask for a magazine held behind the counter of a gas station, and it could only be purchased with a valid ID. Boundaries were good. Now soft core porn is a matter of scrolling social media, reading the news, and the sports page. With the constant use of the internet it's impossible not to see any porn, if not stumble on to hard core porn without trying. Google topics without Safesearch on and watch out. And what does pornography teach us? That the other person is merely momentary property for our pleasure.

The solution? Take up the fight! We will all be tempted, but there is a marked difference between someone who fights against their sin or gives into their sin.

When it comes to porn addiction, I believe it is like many sinful addictions - it is a "vampire sin." "Vampire sins" are named such because they thrive in the dark, and die in the light. Let me explain. In 1 John it is written, "If we **claim to be without sin**, we deceive ourselves and the truth is not in us. If we confess our sins, he is faithful and just and will forgive us our sins and **purify us from all unrighteousness**" (1:8-9). If we deny our sins and do not confess them, like vampires they thrive in the darkness of secrecy. If we confess these sins, the light of God's Word can kill them and help break the addictive power of that sin. The sin of porn addiction is a sin meant to be confessed to a trusted Christian.

Christian community has the gift of confession and absolution. In Christian community we have the opportunity to confess our sins to a trusted Christian, who can share with us the forgiveness Jesus won.[19]

Other Christians were made to help us carry the burden of sin and pray for us.[20]

I'm choosing not to write a diatribe about homosexuality. Here are the cliff notes. It's a sin.[21] It can feel like we were born this way, because we were born with a sinful nature.[22] It's a sin that Jesus paid for.[23] Hallelujah! It's a sin that should be fought against,[24] but like most pet sins it may not be fully conquered until we become perfectly holy in heaven.[25]

But the most glaring problem with this sin today is simply that it is not fought against. The fight or flight position of shame pushed the fighters to center stage. The illogical, ironclad case of defense is this: if you're against this sin, compelled by God's Word, you are not a faithful witness to the God who created sex. Rather, you are a homophobe and a hater. In fact, you cannot claim to care about people who are homosexual. (By the way, as a Christian I love those who struggle with homosexuality, and I do not consider myself morally superior. More than anything I want them to know Jesus' love and forgiveness, and like me strive to honor Him - even though we may fail often). I think you can be a strong believer who is struggling with the sin of homosexuality. But that's not the conversation we've been having in America.

When we choose to handle the gift of sex God's way instead of our way, we will respect the boundaries God set. Whatever they may be, however counter-cultural they may be.

2) Approach marriage as an avenue for holiness.

> "But since sexual immorality is occurring, each man should have sexual relations with his own wife, and each woman with her own husband. The husband should fulfill his marital duty to his wife, and likewise the wife to her husband" (1 Corinthians 7:2-3).

In a sex-crazed society like Corinth, Paul approached the blessing of marriage as an avenue to stay holy. This holiness would give God great glory. Yet Paul also understands the power and intoxication of sex, and so he gives direction. A man and woman should pursue marriage, and offer each other to their partner so that sexual desires find their proper place.

I met with a sex therapist a while back. She gave me a list of love languages and invited me to guess which ones were most important to my wife. I tried picking two out of the ten from her list. I later found out I had guessed wrong, but my wife was gracious in correcting me. Then the therapist said something that stunned me. She said that when a man has sex, he feels all ten love languages at once with a single encounter. Wowzers. The power of sex again. (By the way - not the same for a woman). Many women find the love languages that proceed the act more fulfilling than the act itself.

Speaking in general terms men were built to be physical creatures, and part of that God-ordained physical nature is a strong desire for sex. There is a cyclical nature to the hormones God gave men that mimics the cyclical nature of the hormones that God gave women. Obviously, those hormones guide in different directions and with different desires based on your gender.

What does this mean? Man, you are not a sex-crazed maniac because of your strong desire for sex. Woman, your husband is not trying to take advantage of you, but many times feels most loved by you through sex. By mutually agreeing to regular sex, holiness can be fought for together.

Back to Paul. Paul's suggestion works. Communicate, pray, respect each other, and seek the needs of your spouse. Great sex involves communication, selflessness, and a desire to serve your spouse.

3) View celibacy or periods of abstinence as a gift.

> "I wish that all of you were as I am. But each of you has your own gift from God; one has this gift, another has that" (1 Corinthians 7:7).

The best men I know didn't have sex.

Paul, at least after conversion, called his life of celibacy a gift. He viewed it as an opportunity to be dedicated to God alone, without having his interests divided. As an unmarried man he was able to share the message of the resurrected Jesus across the world in a way that would have been impossible if he were married. God used Paul, and Paul's single state, to change the world with the Gospel.

Jesus, the perfect Lord, led a life of celibacy. He modeled what it was to put the will of the Father first. Make no mistake, He was tempted by the power of sex - for He was tempted in every way.[26] He encouraged companionship and all the gifts of marriage - for He is the Word made flesh.[27] But Jesus, like Paul, had a very specific mission. Jesus understood a married man wouldn't be suited for it.

You and I have, or will have, or have had seasons where we didn't have sex. From the younger years when the desire isn't there. To the ages where we could, but we shouldn't until marriage. Yet, even in marriage where both husband and wife have an understanding of the gift of sex - sex will not always be possible. It could be that your spouse is sick, had a baby, is so not in the mood, was abused and now triggered, or is gone from home for an extended time.

In conversations with many men, I've found different stories but similar circumstances - sex wasn't possible in their marriage for a season. Now, hopefully that season can change, and they can use the powerful uniting gift God gave. But what should godly married men do when they can't have sex?

View minor or extended abstinence as a gift. When your spouse is sick, what is it to take the pressure off in that arena - a gift. When your spouse is exhausted from the busyness of the week, and they just want to go to bed - it's a gift to grant them peace. When your spouse is scared, uncomfortable, and simply needs kindness - it's a gift to use all the other love languages for that day.

But what do you do with your sexual desire during these periods when you can't have sex?

Paul's "thorn in the flesh" is gloriously ambiguous. I'm so thankful we don't know what it was because then we can all relate to it. Every Christian can relate to a struggle we want gone in our life, that we've prayed earnestly about, and isn't going away, yet.

What if the "thorn in his flesh" was his sexual desire, though he chose a celibate life? Paul is the one who said about temptation, "Who is weak, and I do not feel weak? Who is led into sin, and I do not inwardly burn" (2 Corinthians 11:29). Sounds like a man who understands the power of sex. What if Paul's celibacy has less to do with some supernatural spiritual gift, and more about a godly desire to serve God with all his heart while committing to self-control? What if the earnestness of his pleading comes from the intensity of the desire?

Well, it would normalize struggle. It would also give new meaning and hope to God's response, "My grace is sufficient for you, because my power is made perfect in weakness" (2 Corinthians 12:9).

May you know the grace of God is sufficient for you. May you experience the power of the Spirit who grants strength for self-control. May we dwell in the grace of God that has removed our sin as far as the east is from the west.

STUDY QUESTIONS

1) What examples do you have of sex destroying people's lives?

2) How do you currently view sex? Dirty or as a gift of God? In what ways have you seen the power of sex? Agree or disagree, "In marriage sex is one of the most powerful uniting forces."

3) What sexual messages does our society promote that are very harmful? What is God's answer for these messages?

4) How easy is it to access pornography? What help is there to combat porn today?

5) Read Romans 1:21-27. Is God saying homosexuality is sinful from those verses? In what ways have you seen an attempt to excuse the sin of homosexuality? How do we show love to those who struggle with the sin of homosexuality?

6) If married, in what ways have you experienced your spouse is different from you when it comes to sex? What have you found as answers to these God-ordained differences?

7) Have you experienced sexless seasons? What have you found as sources of strength during those times?

MONEY

———⁘———

Kevin McCallister from "Home Alone" is an iconic character. Forgotten by his family at Christmas, not once but twice. Left to fend for himself against the Wet and Sticky Bandits - those lovable goofballs who somehow survive Kevin's gauntlet of pain. Perhaps I love this movie because as a child I found another child hero. Perhaps I love this movie because I love Chicago and it's set in the suburbs - the McCallister house is in Winnetka, Illinois. And there are so many memorable scenes. Kevin with his classic shout after splashing on aftershave, Kevin being reunited with his mom at the end of the movies, Kevin's heart to heart with the bird lady, and the neighborhood grump.

But there is one scene in particular that has stuck with me. In "Home Alone 2" Kevin is in New York City at Duncan's Toy Chest and has this great exchange with the shop owner. He is at the cash register checking out, and Kevin sees a Christmas donation for a children's hospital. Kevin, inspired by the noble cause, uses his dad's money to donate to the children's hospital. As rationale for his actions he says, "The hospital needs the money more than I do, besides, I'm probably going to spend it on stuff that will rot my teeth and my mind."[1]

This sticks with me because Kevin somehow approaches money in a far different way than most people do. He exhibits an "it's not about me" mentality with money. He finds himself merely as a conduit to a greater cause. He sees there's something greater than the pleasure of more toys and candy. He also isn't dealing with his own money, which may or may not have made giving easier.

It's not common to approach money like Kevin in that moment. More common is Kevin in the Plaza Hotel with room service and every dessert on the menu.

Most people have a problem with money. **There may be no "I" in team, but there is a "me" in money**. And most live thinking their money is all about me. We live as if it's in my possession, then it must be for my pleasure. So when the increase comes, let's buy *that* car, *that* house, and go on *that* vacation. After all, it's my money and I deserve it.

I remember Fridays as a bank teller because there was buzz of excitement in the air. Years back, before everyone did electronic banking, people were given physical paychecks (wild, right!?). I had the joy of processing those paychecks, and hearing what people were up to on the weekend. There was great joy as they talked about how they were going to spend their money. I heard where they were going out for dinner, what concert they had planned on, and what sale they were going to snatch up. The buzz in the bank had to do with spending that money on, you guessed it, me.

In contrast there is knee-jerk groaning when money cannot be about me. Think of the loud groaning in this country over taxes. If you want to hear it louder, come to Illinois. Think of the loud groaning kids do when prompted to share their money with their siblings. Think of the groaning in church when the sermon is about money. People give up going to church because the pastor had the audacity to bring up the idea that money is not about me.

Money is a highly personal subject. Trying to catch a glimpse of what someone makes or how they spend their money is a greater sin than little boys trying to glimpse at girl's underwear. The conversation of anyone (even God) telling me what to do with my money has an air of "how dare you!?"

So let's rip this bandaid already, and let me be painfully direct so we can make progress. **Your money is not yours, and my money is not mine - it belongs to God.** Did that hurt? I'm sorry…but not really. I'm more excited to start a greater conversation with the potential to make an eternal difference. I'm more excited to redeem money for something far more important than what's in it for me.

King David is one who called out this concept. He had just given the largest offering to the Lord in recorded history. He was collecting materials for the temple that his son, Solomon, would build for God. He personally gave one hundred and twelve tons of gold, and he inspired the people to give one hundred and ninety tons of gold along with silver, bronze, and precious stones. The gold alone would have been worth over nineteen billion in today's market. If anyone could have been high on himself and his generosity - it could have been David. But he wasn't. Instead he humbly confessed, "But who am I, and who are my people, that we should be able to give as generously as this? **Everything comes from you, and we have given you only what comes from your hand**" (1 Chronicles 29:14).

But people today might argue, "David, it was your money. You fought many battles and conquered many nations to be a rich king. You governed diligently so that there would be money in the storehouse. You had the plan for this offering, and if you didn't, this money would not be here." And David's potential rebuttal, "Who allowed me to win those battles? Who gave me the wisdom to govern and brought the increase? Who is worthy of so much more than what was just given? It is God from whom all blessings flow."

Jesus had a lot to say about money, and it's not because He was holding a fundraiser for a monument in His name. Jesus had a lot to say about money because He loves us, and He knew its potential sway on our hearts. He knows that when it comes to the things vying for our love - money may be number one. So He said, "No one can serve two masters. Either you will hate the one and love the other, or you will be devoted to the one and despise the other. You cannot serve both God and money" (Matthew 6:24). The heart only has room for one top spot, and that spot is reserved for Jesus.

When we approach money with a "it's not about me" mentality, we allow God to retain the number one spot in our hearts.

This conversation leads us into a common misconception about money. Many believe being rich may be sinful. Some Christians might even give off the impression that if you have nice things, your priorities are a mess. The truth is, while they can see your house, they cannot see your level of generosity. Others seem to suggest that true spiritual living would prompt us to eat rice and beans for every meal and live in a van down by the river.

This simply is NOT true. You can be rich and full of faith, as many of the church fathers like Abraham, Jacob, and David proved. You can have nice things, and it may even be that our good Father delights in giving them. You can live in a house with more space than you need. None of these things in and of themselves are evil. You are not more sinful if you are rich and more spiritual if you are poor. Greed and generosity are found in both camps of rich and poor. Frugality can be a mask for greed, and lavish gifts may be evidence of generosity. Like so many Christian choices, it's the heart that matters. Money itself is amoral - it is not inherently evil or good. Just like a baseball bat can hit a ball or hit a neighbor - so money can do a ton of good and cause a ton of harm.

So where does this misconception come from? Let me suggest this verse, "For **the love of money** is a root of all kinds of evil. Some people, eager for money, have wandered from the faith and pierced themselves with many griefs" (1 Timothy 6:10). Did you catch the difference? (I hope the bolding helped). It's not money that is the problem, but the love of money. It's when money has the top spot in your heart that you are pierced with many griefs, and could even wander from the faith.

Grief and the love of money is seen in the American workforce. It's common for many professionals to work fifty to seventy hours. It's common to have a full-time job and a side hustle. It's common to miss weekends and vacations, to miss family time, time for hobbies, and time for God because of the relentless demands of a job. It's common, but is it good? Is it necessary?

A psalm that has the potential to set us free says, "In vain you rise early and stay up late, toiling for food to eat—for he grants sleep to those he loves" (Psalm 127:2). What if instead of running on the hamster wheel in the constant pursuit of more, we got off and started to rest? What does godly rest look like in a world consumed by the pursuit of money?

To get to a state of rest and peace, we must talk about giving.

Let's start with the most positive, primary reason to give money back to the Lord. **The major reason we do anything for the Lord on the other side of His empty tomb is love.**

I have a mom who often said, "I would give you the world if I could." And then she along with my dad would try. As a pastor's family they would get take out us out to eat, they would buy us shoes like Reebok Pumps, and they even took us to Disneyland. Many times I wondered how could they afford to do this. As I grew into adulthood they gifted me a laptop computer for seminary, along with a Daewoo Leganza (that's a car made by a South Korean company) when I got married. My parents proved over and over that love gives, and it tries to give more than it can.

It's something I felt when I fell in love. Falling in love was an investment of time, emotion, and *money*. When it became time to pop the question, I went ring shopping in the diamond district of Los Angeles. I wanted to give more than I had. I wanted a ring to knock the socks off my future bride. I wanted her to feel a level of extravagance with the diamond that hung from her finger. That way, even on the many days I would be a bonehead, she would have evidence that I love her. It's something I felt when I had kids. I've used the same line my mom gave, "I would give you the world if I could. And if it'd be helpful." (Judiciously, I added that last line). And my quest to show lavish love for my girls isn't over yet.

Generously giving back to God is a silent way to shout, "God, I love You! God, you're worth it! God, more than anything I could spend money on, I want to give it to You. See look, You can have it all, along with anything else because I know You've got me!" And God who doesn't need a penny, but simply wants our hearts, is honored by that kind of giving. He knows

68

when a gift is prompted by love. He knows when a generous gift includes trust in His providence.

Consider what Paul wrote to encourage this type of giving, "Each of you should give what you have decided **in your heart to give**, not reluctantly or under compulsion, for God loves a cheerful giver" (2 Corinthians 9:7). As he was encouraging the Corinthian Christians to give, he appealed to their hearts as an opportunity to show love.

Generously giving to God is also a way to release the stranglehold of greed upon our hearts.

The person who dies with the most toys doesn't win, they just die. You can be buried with your possessions, but they won't go with you.

Someone who recognized this principle is Alexander the Great. On his deathbed, he gave a few requests to his generals. One request is that his treasury would be emptied, and the gold, silver, and precious jewels would be scattered on the way to his burial. Another request is that both hands would be dangling out of his coffin. The rationale behind these requests? He wanted the treasures to be scattered to let others know though he spent his whole life filling up the treasury, he can take none of it with him. He wanted his hands visible so others could see he goes to his grave empty-handed. The story goes that his last words were these, "When you bury my body, don't build any momentum and keep my hands outside so that the world knows that the person who won the whole world had nothing in his hand while dying."[2]

The perspective of a dying man is leaving with empty hands. The perspective of a godly man is living with open hands.

I wonder if Alexander the Great stole his cue from Job. Job lost almost every earthly possession in a day, and then declared, "Naked I came from my mother's womb, and naked I will depart. The Lord gave and the Lord has taken away; may the name of the Lord be praised" (Job 1:21). Job knew every gift came from God. Job understood whatever he had in his hand at the time could be taken back by the God who put it there.

Open-handed living understands we could hold in our possession a car, a house, clothes, and kids. Yet, at any time, God can take whatever is in our hand, and replace it with something else. But this is so hard!! So how do we get there?

Sometimes memes speak to me. One meme shows a young girl holding onto a small teddy bear. Jesus with one hand is asking for it, and she doesn't want to give it up. She's tight-fisted about her teddy bear. But the meme shows Jesus with his other hand holding a much bigger teddy bear behind his back. The girl doesn't know that Jesus wants to give her something so much more if she was willing to have open hands.[3] Could that be true for us too? Open hands allow us to have and to hold onto many things, but none too tightly.

How can we go from tight-fisted to open-handed? Generously giving back to God. Generously giving pries the tight grip our hands have on stuff. Stuff is just stuff, but God is God! We recognize this important truth when we are willing to give anything and all things back to Him. This is a regular practice for the generous giver whose regular offerings go beyond that night out, that big screen tv, and that grand vacation. Do you want a heart that isn't gripped by greed because it beats for God? There is no greater cure than generosity.

But there is secondary reason to give. **When we approach money with a "it's not about me" mentality, we become the wisest of managers.**

If we admit that our money is not ours, we find ourselves in the position of managers.

To talk about managing money, let me set up a hypothetical situation. Let's say a mom gives her child twenty dollars to go to the grocery store. She asks the child to pick up a gallon of milk, butter, and two cartons of eggs. Let's say the child comes back from the store with a gallon of milk, butter, two cartons of eggs with the receipt and exact change. Might that mom entrust the child with forty dollars to manage even more of the grocery list? I think so. Yet, what if the child who was given twenty dollars comes back with Pop Rocks, a couple toys, and comic books. There is no receipt, none of the items requested, and no change. Will the mom send the child back with even more money to try it again? I know I wouldn't.

In our personalization of money, we at times forget that God sees how we manage every dime. Even if we were able to hide our earnings and spending from the IRS, we cannot hide it from God. He knows when we are following His directives of financial stewardship, and when we are completely ignoring them. Something sobering to think about is this: why would God over-resource unwise management of what is His? The good news is that in His mercy and grace, the God who feeds birds and clothes flowers still promises to provide for foolish managers. But what if we did what He directed? Is it possible He could bless wise management of what is His? I think it is more than possible, I think it's what He is longing to do.

So what are His directives?

"Whoever sows sparingly will also reap sparingly, and whoever sows generously will also reap generously" (2 Corinthians 9:6).

This verse reminds me of fertilizing the lawn. I remember being at Ace Hardware looking at bags of fertilizer and debating how many I needed. I wondered, "What's the least I can spend here? What could I do with one bag?" Well, one bag could probably make the front yard green. But the better question was, "How much of my lawn do I want to be green?" It might cost more money, but it would lead to a greater result. Eventually, I got used to buying three bags to cover the whole lawn. I found whatever I sow in fertilizer, I'm going to reap with healthy, green grass.

You don't have to be a farmer, or a home landscaper, to find the sowing and reaping principle at play. What you sow in study, you reap in good grades. What you sow in exercise and diet, you reap in health. What you sow in investments, you reap in retirement.

Reaping and sowing is such an important place to start when it comes to money management because of our sinful hearts. Our sinful hearts ask, "What's the least I have to give?"

As a pastor I often hear the question, "Do I have to give 10%?" The tithe is referenced in the Old and New Testament. But the new covenant does not demand a tithe as we considered earlier in the words of Paul. God loves a cheerful giver who gets to decide. Sometimes when people hear this, there is a sigh of relief. "Phew, I didn't have 10% to give. Yay, I can give way less." I get it. I've been there, and I struggle here too. But it's the wrong question with the wrong attitude about the answer.

The real question we should ask when giving is, "How much do I want to reap?" God wants to bless the generous giver. God is literally waiting on us to pour out that blessing. Consider the Proverb that says, "Honor the Lord with your wealth, with the firstfruits of all your crops; then your barns will be filled to overflowing, and your vats will brim over with new wine" (Proverbs 3:9-10).

At our church we did a sermon series called *10 for 10*. The goal was to challenge our church family to give 10% of their income for 10 weeks and see what they found. Years later I heard from a member who tried it, and then continued. She told me she is not only able to keep giving at our church but has since started giving to other noble causes as well. The bottom did not drop out for her finances, and she was convinced God's directives were for her good. We had a chance to reflect, "Isn't God great! His promises are true! And by the way, isn't this fun!?"

I'm not saying you're going to give ten dollars and God is going to give you one hundred somehow. I'm not saying because you give generously, you will become CEO of a Fortune 500 company with all the material possessions you've ever dreamed of. I'm not saying that getting should be our motivation for giving. And I'm not trying to peddle a prosperity gospel for the good of my ministry.

But I am saying God is faithful! I am saying God keeps His promises and blesses first-fruit givers in many and varied ways. I am saying loudly, definitively, and boldly that you cannot out-give the Giver, but you can have a ton of fun trying. Go ahead, I double-dog dare you - try it! Take the 10 for 10 challenge or go beyond!

Real financial peace is possible through generous giving.

I love how Dave Ramsey is helping people with "Financial Peace University." I'd recommend it for those trying to clean up messy financial circumstances. There are some great practical insights on how to manage money. I particularly enjoy the "give, save, live" approach to personal budgeting. I understand the intent that "if you live like no one else, later you can live like no one else."[4] Though Scripture does warn us about planning a future we are not in control of, especially without being generous towards God.[5] Dave Ramsey also appropriately picks up on and emphasizes generosity toward God.

Scripturally speaking though (and I believe David Ramsey would agree), true financial peace doesn't come through a budgeting program. You can budget wisely and go jobless for months beyond an emergency fund. You can save for retirement and spend all your savings on years in a nursing home. True financial peace comes from a heart that trusts in God. Generous, first-fruit giving is a way to such peace. When you plan to give proportionate, generous gifts you are declaring who's got your future. Practically speaking it's also a way to clean up the mess.

This probably sounds all sorts of bad...but when I hear of a friend's financial strain, I often get curious about their level of generosity. I know, I know...it's none of my bees wax. How dare I!? Humbly, I know financial strain comes to generous givers. But I want to go there at least to begin with, because I sincerely want to help. I sincerely want them to be well. And I truly believe generous giving is the starting point, not the afterthought for financial wellbeing. I believe in the sowing and reaping principle and the Giver waiting to bless.

I'll state it again: **When we approach money with a "it's not about me" mentality, we become the wisest of managers.** But even when it comes to wise management, let me declare "it's not about me." Wise management, as it turns out, is also a blessing to those around me.

God has always used the circumstances of history to tell His story. Jesus was born during a period of history called the "Pax Romana" or Roman Peace. Because of the Roman Empire, for about two hundred years, there was safe travel and a common language throughout most of the world.[5] When Jesus rose from the dead, Paul could spread the Gospel like wildfire throughout the world because of the "Pax Romana." Just before Martin Luther unveiled the Gospel of grace in 1517, the printing press was born in the 1400s.[6] When Luther had to prove salvation was by grace alone, through faith alone, in Christ alone - he was helped through that powerful tool. He was able to put in the hands of the people not only his proofs, but the Word of God itself. Today, the United States of America stands as one of the most affluent countries of all time. We are among the richest people who have ever lived, and it's not even close.[7] And we are also a country with the most Christians. According to Pew Research there were about 178 million Christian adults in 2009, in a country that has about 233 million adults.[8]

God used the combination of Paul and the "Pax Romana." God used the combination of Luther and the printing press. What could God do with the combination of riches and Christians in our country?

I was reading an article that asked the question of what would happen to the world if every Christian tithed. Mike Homes estimated there would be an extra one hundred sixty-five billion dollars to manage. Here are some thoughts from the author: twenty-five billion could relieve global hunger, starvation and deaths from preventable diseases in five years. Twelve billion could eliminate illiteracy in five years. Fifteen billion could solve the world's water and sanitation issues, specifically at places in the world where one billion people live on less than one dollar per day. One billion could fully fund all overseas mission work. One hundred billion would still be left over for additional ministry expansion.[9]

That last part geeks me out, and it's not because I'm in ministry looking for a pay raise. Yet because I am in ministry, I know the correlation of giving and sharing God with others. Money is a tool used by God to share the Gospel of Jesus! I've seen time and time again this equation. More giving to God = more sharing of God with others. It's through giving that missionaries are sent and sustained. It's through giving that online communities like Academia Cristo are begun,[10] and then used to train pastors throughout South America. It's through giving that local churches are fully staffed to be an excellent representation of Christ in their community. Funding Gospel ministry is the primary benefit of giving to God that benefits our neighbor.

Yet another great reason to give is to help those in need and be a blessing to others.

Several years back, the financial plight of single parents became clear to me. Talk about financial strain, single parenting is no joke! So I conducted a generosity test. I sent a small gift of forty dollars anonymously through the mail to a single parent. I hoped it would make some difference. Later, I heard from the single mom what an incredible difference this gift made. Forty dollars was enough to get her out of a financial crisis! She was so grateful for this gift! And I was grateful that God used such a small thing to make such a visible difference.

So I learned this lesson clearly: generosity matters for our neighbor. Money is simply a tool that often is given to us but intended for others. We can choose to use money for ourselves, or we can become conduits to a greater cause.

I think this mentality is what inspired the Christians in Corinth. Paul writes about them, "Entirely on their own, they urgently pleaded with us for the privilege of sharing in this service to the Lord's people" (2 Corinthians 8:3-4). What was that privilege? They wanted to give financial aid to other Christians in crisis. They were glad to give it!

At our church we talk about money in a strange way. We don't say we have to give, we say we "get to give." Have-to's are doing the laundry, cleaning the dishes, and taking out the trash. Get-to's are eating ice cream, taking a nap, and going on a vacation. When we see all the blessings God has for us and our neighbor, the simple conclusion is this: **we get to give.**

I think that's how Kevin McCallister felt. It's probably why he fought the bad guys to get those children the money.

I know it's how our God felt. God the Father gave us His world when He gave us His Son. The Son gave us something far greater than money when He shed His blood. And the motivation for all of this? "God so **loved** the world that he gave us his one and only Son" (John 3:16). "For the **joy** set before him he endured the cross, scorning its shame" (Hebrews 12:2).

Love prompts us to give. Giving grants joy. It's the way of our God. Empowered by the Spirit, may it be our way as well.

STUDY QUESTIONS

1) Do you have a hard time spending money on someone other than yourself? How do you feel about the statement, "Your money is not yours"?

2) How have you seen others run after money instead of God? In what ways are you tempted by money? Do you believe generosity is an answer for greed?

3) On a scale of 1-10 how would God rank your management of the money God gave you? Would God use the word "generous" to describe your management? In what ways have you seen a correlation between sowing with God's money, and reaping?

4) Do you agree with Ramsey's approach of budgeting and 1) Give, 2) Save, 3) Live? What percentage of your income are you currently giving back to God?

5) What are the biggest wastes of money? How can money be used to advance the Gospel of Jesus? Is your church fully-funded and firing on all cylinders? What could your church do better at or more of if the funding were there?

6) What is your experience with helping the poor? Would you agree that giving generously to God and to others is a "get-to" versus a "have-to"?

PAIN

God will use you to the degree he breaks you.[1] I heard this statement early on in ministry. I didn't want it to be true. I hoped that God would use me powerfully without any painful ordeals. It didn't happen for me. I now stand convinced that God uses our pain to help others and to point us to Jesus.

I consider Paul's story, or should I say Saul's story. When Jesus appeared with a blinding light on Saul's way to Damascus, Jesus said many things. Jesus wondered why Saul was persecuting him and causing pain for His people. Jesus told Ananias that Saul was His chosen instrument to reach the Gentiles. But something about this account is easy to overlook, yet is so insightful. It's when God says, "I will show him **how much he must suffer** for my name." (Acts 9:16).

What!? I get the first part. Stop creating pain for God's people, Saul. Release the Gentiles from the pain of guilt by sharing Jesus' story, Saul. But suffer for my name, Saul? As a direct result of the calling? How can this be?

Current American culture seeks to escape pain in any way possible. This is seen in our desire for instant gratification. We want products delivered the same day. We want our food our way and on our timeline. (I love watching where my Uber Eats driver is and hoping they'll skip a stop to get to me). We don't want to delay purchases so we use credit to get it now. Escaping pain is also seen in our culture's dependency on substances. The CDC reported, "The number of drug overdose deaths increased by nearly 30% from 2019 to 2020 and has quintupled since 1999."[2] We live in an era they call an Opioid Overdose Epidemic. Avoiding pain and unpleasant circumstances seems to be at the core of the American Dream. We are in such a pursuit of happiness that pain seems nothing more than an obstacle to overcome.

Culture has an insidious way of seeping into Christian life. A conversation about God's specific will in a Christian's life may have cultural underpinnings. The American Dream mentality oozes into believer's lives, perhaps unknowingly. So you might hear something like this, "Well, we decided after much prayer we were going to do _____. But we were met with _____, and it just didn't feel right. So we decided it wasn't God's will. If God were in it, it wouldn't have felt that way." In the end, Christians may feel pain is foreign, and even an enemy to the will of God.

There is much at stake to interpreting pain correctly. Pain presents a fork in the road. Pain will either draw you closer to God, or draw you further from God. Many walk away from God because they can't reconcile His goodness with what He allows. The question that has been labeled the cross of the theologian is, "If there is a good God, why is there so much pain?"

So let's unravel what we can about pain from Scripture, and then see what God's use of it may be.

Pain brings up specific questions to which we have only general answers. When we are in pain we want an explanation. If God allowed a job loss, a mom to get sick, or especially a child to die - we want it to make sense. No, from our sense of justice, we need it to make sense. So Christians say, "when I get to heaven I'm going to ask God about this."

Now in general we know Adam and Eve's fall into sin created pain, and it created chaos that leads to confusion.[3] The chaos sin created should not be underestimated. Because of the fall, we simply will not understand why such great pain is allowed.

Enter Job. Job is impressive. He certainly has a higher seat in heaven than most of us. God said about Job, "he is blameless and upright, a man who fears God and shuns evil" (Job 1:8). Yet, regardless of his right standing through faith, he has tremendous pain. His story proves you can be in a great relationship with God and still suffer greatly. In a day, he loses his incredible wealth and all ten of his children. He would also experience tremendous physical pain, to the degree it felt good to scratch himself with broken shards of pottery. Still, Job is impressive. The decree on Job's reaction to pain is this: "In all this, Job did not sin by charging God with wrongdoing" (Job 1:22).

If anyone deserved an answer and specific rationale to why he suffered, Job seemed a likely candidate. In fact, God did do something remarkable for Job. At the end of his ordeal, God appeared. But instead of giving Job specific answers, God invited Job to consider the awe and majesty of who He is.[4] He received no specific answers for his pain. In fact, most of the book is Job wrestling with his pain, and his "friends" taking potshots at his character.

Pain brings such confusion even the Son of God asked, "Why?" Jesus hangs on a cross. This is the culmination of the plan the Godhead put together from the beginning of time.[5] **Jesus knows why He hangs on the cross.** He is dying for the sins of the world. Yet, the curse of sin and the chaos created by sin is so intense that Jesus cries, "My God, My God **why have you forsaken me**" (Matthew 27:46). So if you have yet to figure out why a period of pain was allowed, you are not alone.

A comforting perspective for the confusion of pain has to do with a weaver's loom.[6] If you've ever seen a weaver's loom, perhaps someone is making a picture of the Neuschwanstein Castle with string, the backside of the loom looks chaotic. The backside of the loom is filled with knots and snarled string - one colored string going there, another going here. The backside of the loom is anything but picturesque. But if you peak to the front side, you can see the beautiful picture those strings of yarn are making. On earth we live on the backside of the weaver's loom. We see the knots and snarled string, but not a beautiful picture. Every now and then God allows us to peep at the front side, showing you the masterpiece He is making through the chaos. But we never see the full picture. We will only see His masterpiece when our faith is complete and we are with our God.[7] (Which is why when we get to heaven we will not ask, "Why?" We will simple say, "Oh, now I see"). Our confidence for this understanding of pain comes from this promise, "And we know that in all things God works for the good of those who love him, who have been called according to his purpose" (Romans 8:28).

Interestingly, God prompts pain for his people. Back to Job's story. Whose idea was it that Job would suffer? God's! He had a conversation with Satan, and God said to him, "Have you considered my servant Job?" (Job 1:8). It's crazy to think that Job's ordeal was God's idea. But that isn't a one off. God also had the idea to put Paul through pain. Consider these words, "I **was given** a thorn in my flesh, a messenger of Satan, to torment me" (2 Corinthians 12:7). Who gave that thorn the flesh? God did!

So God planned pain for Paul and pain for Job. Could the same God plan our pain as well? And why would He? Theologians have wrestled with the causality of certain pain.[8] Was God behind the pain or was sin the cause of the pain? Regardless of causality, we know the pain was allowed to pass through God's hands and touch us. So again, why?

As we begin our discussion on God's use of our pain, I find this quote helpful. "God never wastes pain. He always uses it to accomplish his purpose. And his purpose is for his glory and our good, we can trust him when our hearts are aching or our bodies are racked with pain."[9] Let's hear it again, *God never wastes pain. He always uses it.*

Absorbing pain for someone else is a powerful expression of love.

It was a beautiful day. Spring was in full bloom in the Chicago area. The tulips were up, the grass was green, and our neighbors decided it was time to tend to their landscaping. They trimmed down many plants, including a bush close to our house where my daughter Bella was playing. My wife was talking to our neighbors enjoying the beautiful weather, and unexpectedly Bella fell. Bella was a toddler at the time, and toddlers fall all the time - it's like they have constant sea legs. Unfortunately for Bella, she fell straight into the freshly trimmed bush of our neighbor, and a branch punctured her cheek. This event signaled our first family trip to the Emergency Room. When we got to the Emergency Room we wanted help pronto, but there was a two hour wait. We were sitting in the lobby of the Emergency Room, holding a cloth to Bella's bleeding cheek, when a very clear and strong sensation came over me. I wanted to switch spots with Bella. In my heart of hearts I thought, "God, puncture my cheek, not hers. She's beautiful, and I'm a dude. Let me wait, not her. God, please can I switch and take the pain from my daughter Bella." Of course I couldn't switch, and God used that pain to shape my daughter. She now has what looks like a dimple because of it. But here's what I found about parental love: parental love is willing to absorb pain for our kids so they don't hurt.

Our God is a perfect parent with perfect love. The Psalmist David says, "As a father has compassion on his children, so the Lord has compassion on those who fear him" (Psalm 103:13). In love, God's plan was to absorb the pain meant for us, so we could be set free.

Jesus' pain was not about Him, it was about us. He could make the switch and absorb what we deserved. Jesus is referred to as "the man of suffering, and familiar with pain."[10]

This always reminds me of people who had a hard life. Do you know anyone like that? I think of my Grandpa Merle Zastrow. He was orphaned as a child. His mother died, and his dad couldn't take care of the kids. He was the eldest sibling looking after the younger ones in a home that was not his own. He was a WWII veteran. He worked hard in a factory. Life wasn't so easy. Now, to a certain degree we know we all will have hardships because of this sinful world. And because we've continued in the sin of Adam and Eve, we are not immune.

Jesus had a hard life. But unlike us, it had nothing to do with what He did. All of His suffering and all of His pain was because of us and what we did. He takes upon Himself what we deserved! He died so we could live. He suffered so we could be set free. In doing so, He absorbed our pain out of love for us. He was able to do what I couldn't do with Bella - switch places. Never is this more clear than through the words of Isaiah. Consider:

"Surely **he took up *our* pain**
  and **bore *our* suffering**,
yet we considered him punished by God,
  stricken by him, and afflicted.
But **he was pierced** for *our* **transgressions**,
  he was crushed for *our* **iniquities**;
the **punishment** that brought *us* **peace** was on him,
  and **by his wounds *we* are healed**.
We all, like sheep, have gone astray,
  each of us has turned to our own way;
and **the Lord has laid on him**
  the iniquity of *us* all" (Isaiah 53:4-6).

If the purpose of Jesus' pain wasn't about Him, what if the purpose of our pain is not about us? **Yes, what if when it comes to pain, "it's not about me"?**

This understanding is what I find in the early Christians when it comes to their pain. There is a story in the book of Acts where the Christians were rounded up by the authorities for preaching about Jesus' resurrection. They were put into prison, and they were flogged. Neither of those things are easy or light. And yet as a reaction to all this, Scripture records, "The apostles left the Sanhedrin, **rejoicing** because they had been counted worthy of suffering disgrace for the Name" (Acts 5:41). They **rejoiced** in their pain, because they knew their pain had come as a direct result of their love for Jesus.

My pain is not about me, it's about my love for Jesus.

Here are the expectations Jesus set for pain. "Whoever wants to be my disciple must deny themselves and take up their cross and follow me" (Matthew 16:24). We are not promised only good all the time, or a pain free existence - we are promised a cross for following Jesus. But just as His cross spoke of His love for us, so our crosses can speak of our love for Him.

My mother told a story about her friend who was an organist. She was one of the only musicians at her church and playing the organ was incredibly stressful for her. When practicing she had to take her young kids along, and while flipping music make them behave. Playing organ meant adding yet another thing to an already busy schedule. And perhaps worst of all, every time she would play her whole body and her hands would shake from the tremendous nerves of playing for the congregation. One of her sons took notice of this and asked, "So Mom, why do you play the organ for church?" And the answer? Because she loved Jesus.

Early on as a pastor, I asked my dad, who is a pastor, "Was pastoral ministry always this hard?" I was talking to my dad about some pressures of the ministry. Along the way I was cheered on by my parents and others for ministry, but I never really saw nor could have prepared for the intense trials that came with it. When the cheering ended and the trials began, the question appeared. I'll never forget his response. He said, "We knew it was tough, but we did it anyway." Why? Because of love for Jesus.

What cross or trial has God allowed as direct result of following Him? Is it the Sunday morning madness? Trying to get the kids to church, with one complaining, one crying, and one throwing up. Is it the sacrifice of volunteering? You see all the other things you could be doing, but the church needs you. Is it trying to be generous? You consider all the other things your offering could buy. And you wonder, "Why am I doing this?" And here is a great answer: love for Jesus.

Yet, there is another reason God allows our pain. **My pain is not about me, it's about understanding the love of Jesus.**

We are saved by grace, and that grace is a gift. Salvation through grace as a gift of God is the great message we proclaim!

When it comes to being given a gift, I love to teach that any payment takes the essence of a gift away. For example, if someone is offering you the latest iPhone as a gift and also requires fifty dollars to receive it - that iPhone is not yours as a gift, but as a discount. Likewise, if we are to proclaim salvation by grace as a gift, yet require any other work - it is not a gift of grace. It is still a salvation by works, no matter how small that work might be. So we are proud proclaimers of salvation that is free because of the gift of Christ Jesus.

But though salvation is free to us, it was not free. Jesus paid a steep price for our salvation. His body was broken and His blood was shed, so we could be redeemed.

COVID-19 rocked our world. Everyone experienced some kind of pain. People dealt with disrupted plans and cancellations. People dealt with financial strain and job loss. People experienced great sickness and even had to deal with death.

I remember reflecting after this collective experience of pain. This was my reflection on pain as it relates to what Jesus did for us. How can we ever truly know Jesus and the length of His love unless we have similar experiences? So He allows physical pain, emotional pain, and relational pain. Why? So we can know and consider a love beyond all reasonable measure. He endured the highest forms of physical pain, emotional pain, and relational pain - all out of love for us. Salvation is free to us, but it was not free. Love cost Jesus dearly, but He gladly paid the price.

"When you're a parent, you will understand." Ever heard that? Isn't it interesting that you never really know what your parents did for you until you become a parent. I mean, it's amazing that life goes on generation after generation when you see what it takes to raise an infant. The sleepless nights, the 24/7 neediness, and the emotional toll is crazy! You can't understand that level of sacrifice until you do it yourself. So much about our parents is uncovered when we do it ourselves. We see how difficult it is to discipline, how hard it is to say no when you want to say yes, and ultimately how you would do anything for your kids.

Like understanding our parents through experience, perhaps we understand the lavish love of Jesus the more we experience pain like His. When friends betray us because of our faith – we can remember how Jesus' disciples deserted Him. When we experience physical pain and abuse – we can remember Jesus bore a crown of thorns and was flogged for us. When we cry out in desperation with anxious hearts – we can bring to mind Jesus praying so intensely He was sweating drops of blood. How else can we know a love so wide and high, so deep and long? Our pain reminds us of Christ's costly love.

When we are in pain and lift our eyes to Jesus, we find the One who suffered so much more for our sake, and we are astounded that any love would bear so much for our sake!

My pain is not about me, it's about pointing others to the love of Jesus.

I was riding in the car with Bella with what was probably bronchitis in my lungs. Snow was on the ground as we traveled, and I felt awful. If there was an option B, I would have taken it. But there wasn't. I was up for a marriage retreat as the main speaker, and I had a sermon to preach the next day. There was no alternate speaker planned for either engagement. All I could hope for was strength for the next moments, and not too many uncontrollable, unstoppable, hacking-a-lung, coughing fits. Thankfully, and by God's grace, I made it through. Weeks later, my daughter reflected and said she was proud of me for making it through. I realize she had a learned a valuable lesson about gutting it out. Through my lens, all I could see was the task in front of me and wishing I'd feel better. Through her lens, she was seeing a dad try to pull it together because work needed to be done. I believe my pain was not about me, but God used it for my daughter.

Much of our pain isn't exclusively for us, it is ours to share. Especially when it comes to the lessons we've learned and how God got us through. I often consider one of the primary reasons Jesus ascended into heaven and gave the work of the church to flawed humans, is so there is a level of relatability. We are holding treasure in jars of clay.[11] And when people see cracks in us, the message of Jesus' love has a way of shining through. And they can see the beauty isn't about us, it's all about Jesus.

So our weakness is a window, and what once was our misery can become our ministry.

So God allows anything and everything. He allows the worst of the worst. He allows abuse, neglect, betrayal, death, financial hardship, sickness, and why? Because someone else will experience those things too. And with

God by your side, you get to point them to the love that gets us through, to the love that sustains us.

Small groups are some of the most powerful environments for the people of God. As a host of small groups for years, I have seen countless people grow in faith and grow close to one another. One of the most galvanizing moments for any group is when a member of the group shares a struggle, and then another member says, "I know what you're talking about! I've been there!" I've seen this happen when it comes to cancer, social anxiety, divorce, and more. Christians helping other Christians not in spite of, but because of the pain they have been through. Christians who give others hope that they too can make it through. Christians who share the most powerful, empathic words one can hear - which are, "You are not alone."

There is no doubt about it, God has a purpose for our pain. He doesn't waste pain; He always uses it. But many times we can say about pain, "it's not about me." It's about knowing Christ's love and sharing that costly love with others.

STUDY QUESTIONS

1) In what ways does our society seek to avoid pain? Do you believe God can use pain for good? Why or why not?

2) Do you remember a season of suffering where you asked, "Why"? Did God allow you to see an answer at some point?

3) If you are a parent, have you ever wanted to take the pain of your child? What pain did Jesus take on for us?

4) If you are a parent, did becoming a parent make you appreciate your parents? How? In what ways did Jesus' suffering for us go further than our own? Is there an area of suffering where you don't think Jesus understands?

5) Have others learned about God through your suffering? How can you point people to Jesus through the pain you have experienced?

CHURCH

My first assignment from Wisconsin Lutheran Seminary was to start a church. I had no idea what it would take to plant a church. In eight years of schooling, I didn't take a class on it. So this was going to be one grand adventure where I needed to lean on God for everything. Early on, we had core group meetings in our living room or in the basement of our friend's condo. We hoped and dreamed and prayed for God's kingdom to come through us. We talked about who we might reach with a church in this area. We talked about the kids, grandkids, husbands, and neighbors who might come to know Jesus through our church, Amazing Love.

As we considered what it would take to reach people with the Gospel of Jesus, one thing became increasingly obvious. **The major road block for the church would be an "it's all about me" mentality.**

It started with me. I was out of my comfort zone straight out of the gate. The Mission Board over me required door-to-door canvassing five nights a week. Have you ever knocked on a stranger's home and tried to strike up a conversation about Jesus? It pumps up your adrenaline, and it takes courage and the ability to take many forms of rejection. It is also very much NOT comfortable. A few times, the neighbors called the police and

I had to convince them I was a pastor and not a crazy person. (Though at the time our church wasn't worshipping and didn't even have a name). This wasn't all that was uncomfortable. It was about starting a business with land and facilities, with a mission, vision, core values, and a location. It required recruiting as many people as possible to follow you on a grand adventure without a finite destination and a ton of faith in God.

When I envisioned being a pastor, I envisioned preaching and teaching. I envisioned hospital and shut-in visits. (Especially, with elderly grandmothers so excited to hear a devotion and to share coffee and cookies with me). I envisioned a building and an office, and perhaps most importantly, a group of people who were eager to have me serve them. That was comfortable, that was my training, and this was not that.

But it was also beautiful, wonderful, and supremely good. It was the type of adventure I imagine the disciples of Jesus must have felt when Jesus said two simple words, "Follow me."[1] They didn't ask where, they simply followed. **Some of the best journeys of faith are with a very clear command of God and a very unclear destination.** Think on the call of Abraham, the anointing of David, the call of Isaiah, the announcement to Mary. Abraham had no clue what land he was being called to and what God would make out of his family line. David had many obstacles and adventures before he would become king. Isaiah in his childhood couldn't have known his words would be the most rich and clear about the coming Messiah. And when Mary was told she would give birth to the Messiah, the wild ride began. They all had very clear commands from God without the destination firmly in mind. They didn't know how the story was going to unfold - they simply had a command to follow.

To take journeys of faith, you have to get comfortable being uncomfortable.[2] You have to embrace the "it's not about me" mentality.

Yet, the local church often strives for comfort over God's calling. The local church is often filled with selfishness over the selflessness required to accomplish God's mission.

Consider a few examples with me. It's no secret that 70-85% of people who visit church for the first time came through a personal invitation.[3] Personal invitation is the most powerful weapon in the arsenal of outreach to extend God's kingdom to many more. Yet, when is the last time you personally invited someone to your church? Church is filled with family and friends for many, and so it is common to catch up with them on Sunday mornings. But who is going to greet the guests? What happens when a guest dare takes the row that your family usually sits in? Congregations may say they have a huge zeal for outreach, and want as many people as possible to know Jesus through their ministry. But if accomplishing that task requires change or sacrifice, many congregational members put up the stop sign signaling, "We've never done that! We could never do that!" And what do personal invitation, greeting new people, and congregational change require? Getting comfortable being uncomfortable.

None of this is easy, none of it comes naturally, and all of it requires us to die to self.

So let's get our bearings for God's desire in the church. The Great Commission is God's desire for the church's activity. Before Jesus ascended into heaven, He gave His people one great command, "Go and make disciples of all nations, baptizing them in the name of the Father and of the Son and of the Holy Spirit, and teaching them to obey everything I have commanded you" (Matthew 28:19-20).

Every good, Bible-believing church has this as part of its mission statement. They may cleverly rephrase these words to make them memorable. Perhaps you even know your church's mission statement. The Great Commission has two main facets of activity. The first is to "go" and do outreach. So churches canvass, invite their friends, host outreach events like VBS, Easter Egg Helicopter Drops, and help the community. The second facet of the Great Commission is to "teach everything." So it is important that there are many paths and opportunities at church to grow in the knowledge of all God has to say - whether it be a small group system, Bible Class, or a mixture of both. The journey of discipleship is never-ending. It's a continual progression of learning and growing. It's work that God does through His church.

At Amazing Love, we've rephrased the Great Commission to say that we are here *to reach the lost with the love of Christ.* This statement obviously emphasizes the "go" facet of the Great Commission. Yet, baked into it is the understanding that as you "go," you will also want to be growing in the understanding of all things God has taught. As you invite people, you will want to sit by them and answer their questions. You will want to be involved in the church to make it the best place possible to hear the Gospel of Jesus. As you get involved in the community you will want to know how to share your faith with them. Going and growing go hand in hand, and both are necessary.

The question is how do we best fulfill the Great Commission? You guessed it. "It's not about me" has to be part of it.

The Great Commission is the principle given by Scripture, but 1 Corinthians 9:22 is the paradigm of how it is done. In 1 Corinthians 9:22, Paul, the greatest missionary of all time, who knew a thing or two about reaching people with the message of Jesus said, "To the weak I became weak, to win the weak. I have become all things to all people so that by all possible means I might save some." For Paul, reaching people wasn't about him! It was about him becoming what people need to see Jesus. Sometimes he blended in with the Jews and operated by their customs.[4] Other times he preached based on the location and cultural preferences around him.[5] Still other times he vigorously defended his ministry so that the message of that ministry would not be lost.[6] He did whatever it took so as many people as possible heard the message of Jesus and his love.

This is still the path forward. It's about dying to self, being comfortable being uncomfortable, and doing whatever it takes so that people see Jesus through us.

Let's dig in and talk about three areas where "it's not about me" is so important for the church.

1) Essentials vs. preferences

Imagine a mom is making a meal for the family. Mom happens to be from New Orleans and makes the best pot of gumbo known to man. The gumbo is ready with Crystal sauce on the side, and the family comes down for supper. First one to the table is the two-year-old son, and he asks if it's mac and cheese because that's what he wants. Sister comes down and hopes it's Taco Tuesday, and is not too excited to see gumbo instead of guac. The eldest is always hungry and says he's so hungry he could eat an entire pizza - so he isn't thrilled with soup. Dad usually eats anything and loves his wife's cooking, but tonight he had a tough day and lets out he could have gone for a big, juicy steak. The gumbo is perfection and everyone is bickering about their meal preference instead of voicing appreciation. Now imagine outside their house, no one has any food. It's a time worse than the Depression era food lines, and everyone is starving. If that's the case, how ridiculous is a family argument over perfectly good food? Beyond ridiculous, it's out of place. It doesn't make sense given the circumstances.

When church life goes wrong, it's about bickering over food preference versus sharing the meal. R.C. Sproul put it this way: "Evangelism is just one beggar telling another beggar where to find bread."[7] If your church is preaching the message of Jesus, share the meal. Your church might serve it up different than the church down the street (gumbo vs. burgers), but we live in a world of beggars starving for this spiritual food. So the real problem to solve in church isn't if the meal is to my preference, as much as how do we get this meal to others.

Now, preference isn't a bad thing. I'm hoping you love the things your church does. I'm hoping the music gives you goosebumps, the preaching feeds you well, and the ministries selected serve you and your family well. I'm praying they are first and foremost true to God's Word, and if not, I would advise looking for a new church. But what I also recognize is there is no perfect church that will suit your every preference. I bet right now even at a great church you still have this thought, "I love my church, but it would be even better if…"

About preferences. Here's a bold statement: Not everyone loves or even likes your preference. I would wager your preferences are different than your parents, neighbors, and even your spouse.

If you don't believe me, try this exercise. Poll five of your closest family and friends and ask them their favorite song to sing in church. My guess is that you'll hear of five different songs based on five different preferences. After that, ask them about their favorite preacher. You'll hear different names. Styles and word choices, even approaches, might differ greatly in the same way gumbo is in no way like a burger. But let's be honest, gumbo and burgers are both delicious. So also, God is glorified through many different voices, many different songs, and many different styles.

I grew up and went to seminary during the worship wars. Which style is better? Can we really use drums and different styles of music? For years our church body has used the liturgy in the form of the Western Rite. Most of the churches in our fellowship are liturgical. And it's beautiful. The liturgy is filled with God's Word, so it's really hard to argue with. There is a richness to a tradition that links Christians together for five hundred plus years. But is something new or non-liturgical bad? Is it inherently less than or perhaps even heretical? Will changing style lead to a change in the substance?

If you think it is a change going from organ music to a praise band, or to move from the assigned readings of the pericope to a sermon series, take a journey with me to the early Christian Church.

The early Christian Church had the essentials. The message of Christ and Him crucified. They knew salvation was through faith in this crucified and resurrected Lord. And this was the message spread throughout the world, especially through the ministry of Paul. Christians would gather regularly to read God's Word, to receive communion, pray, and worship.[8] We don't know what songs they sang, the order of worship, or how long the sermon was. We do know it looked different from place to place. Some worshiped in synagogues like in Jerusalem and some in homes.

The early Christian Church had to wrestle with what style was allowed, and what was forbidden. Things came to a head at the council of Jerusalem. All the big leaders were there: Peter, Paul, and the brother of Jesus named James. They were debating whether they were going to require all the ceremonies of the Old Testament including circumcision. The Pharisees said, "The Gentiles must be circumcised and required to keep the law of Moses" (Acts 15:5). That, by the way, meant a lot of laws beyond circumcision. It included laws concerning clean and unclean foods, it meant required pilgrimage to Jerusalem, and a system of sacrifice. Read Leviticus and you'll start to see all the laws involved in the Old Covenant.

Peter spoke first. He said, "Why do you try to test God by putting on the necks of Gentiles a yoke that neither we nor our ancestors have been able to bear? No! We believe it is through the grace of our Lord Jesus that we are saved, just as they are" (Acts 15:10-11). Peter understood that the laws of the Old Testament were a foreshadowing, the sacrifices a foreshadowing, and the fulfillment was in Christ. He was advocating for a system that emphasized the grace of God over the laws of God.

James, the brother of Jesus, spoke next. He addressed the issue so clearly saying, "It is my judgment, therefore, that we should not make it difficult for the Gentiles who are turning to God" (Acts 15:19). James pointed out that requiring surgery for any male convert would be difficult. Beyond that, the many ceremonial laws of the Old Testament were difficult and were only meant to show us the law-keeper Jesus Christ.

So James concluded, "Instead we should write to them, telling them to abstain from food polluted by idols, from sexual immorality, from the meat of strangled animals and from blood" (Acts 15:20). Basically, tell the Gentiles not to sin or give the impression of idolatry. No rules for worship. No pilgrimage to Jerusalem. No clean and unclean foods and especially no circumcision. And this decision was a watershed moment for the Christian Church. For thousands of years there was one form of worship. And now? In a word, it was free.

Paul confirms this thought of freedom when writing to Christians in Colosse saying,

> "Therefore do not let anyone judge you by what you eat or drink, or with regard to a religious festival, a New Moon celebration or a Sabbath day. These are a shadow of the things that were to come; the reality, however, is found in Christ" (Colossians 2:16-17).

So can there be different forms of music? Consider what the Psalmist said,

> "Praise him with the sounding of the trumpet, praise him with the harp and lyre, praise him with timbrel and dancing, praise him with the strings and pipe, praise him with the clash of cymbals, praise him with resounding cymbals" (Psalm 150:3-5).

As a band geek who played the tuba, I've never come across the lyre, but the Psalmist says it's good for worshiping the Lord. As a German Lutheran, dancing seems like an inappropriate form of worship, yet the inspired writer says dancing is allowed. And if you didn't catch on, the Psalmist doesn't just allow percussion like cymbals, but says they should resound!

So after all this, I have a question. Does your church do anything that makes it difficult for unbelievers to turn to God? If so what is it? And what is stopping you from making the change to eliminate that obstacle? It may take time, money, and advocacy, but don't give up on the desire to make the Gospel as accessible as possible for a dying world that needs Jesus. He is the Bread of life!

I have another question. Why do so many church people give off the impression of sin when it comes to the use of Christian freedom in worship?

This reminds me of a time when the Pharisees reprimanded Jesus on how He practiced the Sabbath. They asked Jesus bluntly, "Why are you doing what is unlawful on the Sabbath" (Luke 6:1). What boldness! How unexpected! To claim the Author of the Sabbath is breaking the Sabbath! They were upset that His disciples were getting food to eat and that Jesus was considering healing a man. So he responded, "I ask you, which is lawful on the Sabbath: to do good or to do evil, to save life or to destroy it" (Luke 6:9).

How did the Pharisees get there, and what is the word of caution? **Be careful not to make men's rules equivalent to God's rules.** We call this legalism, and it's so easy to fall into. The Pharisees were masters of adding more rules to God's rules. At its best, legalism is the result of passion for God and a safeguard for the truth. If a few extra rules guard God's rule, then perhaps those rules are ok, right? At its worst, legalism is a person's attempt to push their preference and avoid uncomfortable circumstances that might result if change is allowed. Regardless of intention, legalism binds the consciences of the weak and restricts where God allows freedom.

Is there anything right now you say is a sin that God does not say is a sin? Have you ever been tempted to push your preference - to the point of it being a law that none dare break? What lies at the heart of this? If it is at all an attempt to guard you from getting uncomfortable from the change that results, it may not be good. If it is an attempt to guard the good things of God, be careful that you are not binding consciences with personal, regional, or generational preference.

Because the essentials of church life are clear. As church people, we must be going and growing (Matthew 28:19-20). We must teach the Bible with doctrinal precision, as any false teaching hurts God's people (1 Timothy 4:16, 2 Timothy 2:17-18). We must seek Jesus as the Savior we need and the world needs (John 1:29, John 14:6). We must not be afraid to confront the sins of our age with God's laws (2 Timothy 4:3), and offer the abounding forgiveness and grace God offers through the cross of Jesus (Psalm 103:11-12). We must remember that any style, form, or artistic expression is a servant to the Gospel of Jesus (1 Corinthians 10:23). If you have a guitar, organ, piano, cymbals or resounding cymbals, may they all be in praise of God (Psalm 150). We must worship in an orderly way that makes the preaching of the Gospel both bold and clear (1 Corinthians 14:40). We must go to worship not to seek more of ourselves, but more of God (Psalm 61:2). He alone is worthy of all praise (Psalm 145:3).

2) Heart vs. empty ritualism

One of the greatest obstacles to God-glorifying worship is going through the motions or checking the box. There are some who might even think just showing up is what God wants, regardless of what they get out of worship. The reality of worship is you can be present without being present. God wants so much more for you and your family than empty ritualism.

Consider these words from Isaiah, "These people come near to me with their mouth and honor me with their lips, but their **hearts** are far from me. Their worship of me is based on merely human rules they have been taught" (Isaiah 29:13).

The same problems in the church were present more than 2700 years ago! Human tradition was clouding the truth. The people of God were present with their bodies, their lips, and even their offerings - but they were not truly present. And God couldn't stand it! He wanted His people to do so much more than check the box and go through the motions.

God said, "Stop bringing meaningless offerings! Your incense is detestable to me. New Moons, Sabbaths and convocations—I cannot bear your worthless assemblies" (Isaiah 1:13).

Can you imagine God showing up to your church and saying, "Stop it! I cannot stand what you are doing!"? It's not what we would expect God to say, especially about giving an offering or singing a song of praise.

Yet, consider it this way. Let's consider an afternoon with your best friend getting coffee. You can't wait to share what's going on in your life, especially with your new boyfriend. But when she arrives, you can tell she didn't get much sleep the night before. And every time you try to share something important, she is dozing off. You ask her questions to see if she has caught anything you said about a recent date, but she hasn't. She doesn't even remember that your boyfriend's name is Brad, though you mentioned his name at least fifteen times. This interaction doesn't build your relationship - it actually tears it down.

Does God know how attentive you are to Him in worship? Of course He does. He desires to be the most important relationship we have on the planet. He desires so much more than the leftovers of our time, attention, talent, and treasures. He desires all that we have and all that we are.

And the radical truth about this desire? It's not because He needs anything from us. It's not because our praise and offerings and attention build Him up, like some insecure friend. **No, He wants our everything because He gave us His everything.** He gave us His heart before we had a chance to give Him ours. Out of love, He sent His one and only Son to bleed and die so we could know joy, forgiveness, and peace. And grace upon grace, He wants to give us more.

In Communion, He wants us to experience a transcendent peace. So He gives us His body and blood in the bread and wine for forgiveness.[9] In Baptism, He wants us to be made new, and so He offers any and all to come and receive a washing of rebirth and renewal.[10] And as we hear His Word in worship, we receive gift after gift. He grants new perspective, new joy, new direction, new reasons for adoration and praise. In worship, we receive priceless gifts that He can't wait to give us again and again.

One of my favorite things that happens in worship is what I call the "funk flip." If during the week I was depressed, stressed out, angry, or anxious - worship does something. I can come to worship in a funk and hearing about my Savior Jesus flips my heart. I don't leave the same way I came in. I don't feel the same. Worshiping the Lord is the greatest remedy to a long standing funk that I know of. And it should be, for we find in worship the greatest Wonder this world has to offer. The Psalmist said, "Lead me to the rock that is higher than I" (Psalm 61:2). We find that rock in Jesus. In worship, Jesus takes our attention off of ourselves and our problems, and He turns it to His power, His love, and His plan for us.

So how do we make sure not to miss the gifts God has for us week in and week out?

When I say about worship, "it's not about me," I can worship God in almost any environment that teaches his truth.

Some of you are students or remember your time as a student. When it comes to getting an A in class, whose responsibility is that? Is it the student's or teacher's responsibility? There are many subjects, some that are preferred, and some that don't relate to your interests at all. There are many teachers and professors, some who you gel with, and some whose thought patterns seem as untraceable as a cat's activity at 2am. But the experience of the classroom is always the same. Regardless of subject material, or the type of teacher - it is the student's responsibility to get an A. So, a student tries hard to know what the teacher expects. He tries hard to pay attention to teachers, who might even annoy him, so that the grades are good.

I bring this up because there is a great correlation between a good student and good worshiper. A good worshiper knows the responsibility of God-glorifying worship is up to him or her. The heart the worshiper brings is more important than the worship environment.

A worshiper bringing his or her heart can see God in almost any preacher and preaching style. The preacher doesn't have to be about me.

Preachers are not the power, God's Word is.[11] Preachers simply echo the truths found in the Bible boldly and clearly.[12] Every preacher is simply a foolish thing of the world that God uses to shame the wise.[13] Every preacher should consider himself nothing, knowing it is God building His Church through the Word.[14]

Yet, we live in an age of "rockstar" preachers. Truly, there are some gifted communicators who relate God's Word in a phenomenal way. Praise God for that, and what a blessing they are to God's Church. But what if your current pastor doesn't have the gifts of communicating like those "rockstars"? What if your current pastor is your dad's preaching preference, or you mom's preaching preference? What if your current pastor is tapering his approach to reach the next generation and loses you with illustrations and references at times?

I would suggest it is still your job to get something out of it as a worshiper who brings his or her heart to see Jesus. Do not let your preference of communication stand in the way of hearing God's truth. Some preachers are intellectuals, and some are creatives. Some are passionate, and some very calm. Some preachers use illustrations and some do not. Some ask for congregational engagement, and some are distracted if you react with an amen. Some have preached for years, and some are just beginning. But all good preachers want you to know God and His love deeply. All good preachers understand they will be judged more strictly as a teacher and want to be a faithful ambassador.[15] And if you put in the work, most times, you can see God through many styles and voices.

A worshiper bringing his or her heart can praise God regardless of musical style. The music doesn't have to be about me.

I've been in the most traditional environments you can imagine, with a procession of the cross, incense, and classical instrumentation. I've been in the most contemporary worship environments you can imagine, where the bass of the percussion shakes your stomach, and they offer ear plugs as you enter. Sometimes the words of the music are so rich, I need to look over the lyrics when the song is done. Sometimes the idea of the lyric is so essential, it repeats again and again. There have been rich phrases in hymns five hundred years old, and rich lyrics in songs that came out five days ago. There has been repetition in the liturgy and repetition in a contemporary song's refrain. Sometimes I find myself thinking this musical style must be the style of heaven, and other times I wonder if this style is anyone's true preference besides the artist who created it.

Regardless of musical style, I make it my responsibility to praise God from my heart. Sometimes that includes doing my best on the bass line of the four-part harmony. Sometimes it's singing loud enough to hear my voice over the stomach shaking bass. Sometimes it's silently appreciating an artist's riff on the organ, or guitar. And yes, sometimes according to my sinful nature the style is so different I find myself complaining. But that often has more to do with me than if the style or song was acceptable or not.

When we get to heaven with perfect faith, I believe the distraction of different styles will cease. On earth, we may have to get over ourselves and blend in with the environment created.

A worshiper bringing his or her heart will not need to be spoon-fed, but will learn discernment. The interpretation of the environment can be filled with grace and guarded by truth.

Preachers get it wrong. Most don't try to. If you have noticed they are a false teacher, seek a different church pronto. But sometimes good preachers say the wrong thing, the unclear thing, or a misleading thing. As a preacher, I remember that if it's unclear in my mind, it will be a cloud to the congregation.

Many times, I see the Holy Spirit at work. Amazingly, people will approach me after a sermon and tell me a point they got from the sermon...that I didn't make! Thankfully, the Spirit is at work clearing up what I made cloudy.

If I take in a message with a fault-finding spirit, trust me, I can find mistakes in anyone. If something was unclear, I can label them a false teacher and have reason to make it an issue. Yes, I too can play the devil's advocate. At the same time, if I take in a message with grace, seeking the right interpretation, I can often understand what was otherwise unclear. I prefer giving grace and assuming the best. Most preachers are doing their best to be faithful to God's Word of truth. I'd strongly caution you against needlessly arguing with your spiritual leaders. Actually, God would too.[16]

I remember it is **my responsibility** to retain the truths of God's Word. I remember this as I consider the Berean Christians. They heard Paul preach. And instead of letting what Paul said stand (who, by the way, was pretty clear and reliable) - they investigated. Look what is said about them: "Now the Berean Jews were of more noble character than those in Thessalonica, for they received the message with great eagerness and examined the Scriptures every day to see if what Paul said was true" (Acts 17:11).

The interpretation for the Bereans didn't stop on Sunday morning. They made sure Paul's teaching stood up to Scripture. And because they did that, they would not be rocked by false teaching, and they would be edified by the truth. Interpretation wasn't reliant on the strength of the preacher's points or charisma, it was reliant on their knowledge of Scripture.

A Christian should not stand for repeated false teaching and should seek a new church.[17] Yet, a Christian also should not have his or her faith swayed by false teaching. The goal of a mature Christian should be to enter any Christian environment being able to discern truth from false teaching. We must be Berean Christians who know how to fight for the truth, especially with our access to so much Christian content.

A great example of what this looks like has to do with "The Chosen." Have you seen this TV series? I personally love that other Christians are trying to make the Bible come to life. What a God-glorifying venture! But because they are telling the story apart from a verse by verse approach, there is the need to fill in gaps with artistic expression. There is artistic expression in the way Jesus walks and talks and in the characterizations of the disciples. Some people love it! Some people don't agree with it. And some people don't like it at all. But if we are like the Berean Christians, we should be able to take it in, discern what is from God and what is art. The series should not be the basis for our faith in Jesus, nor should it tear from it.

3) Contributor vs. consumer

Perhaps the foundation for this whole mentality approaching the church saying, "it's not about me" has to do with being a contributor versus a consumer at the local church.

Did you know that God wants to make use of you at your local church? He describes your activity as so important, if you are not involved it's like a body missing a hand or an eye.[18] **God made you on purpose for a purpose.** That doesn't just include things outside the church - it also includes your involvement inside the church.

Serving at the church is so important that at Amazing Love we say, "if you're not serving, you're swerving." Basically, it means you will feel disconnected to your church if you're not involved. More than that, you will feel disconnected to your Savior, as service inside the church is an integral part of the faith.

Think about serving this way.

If you are invited over to a Thanksgiving meal where one person makes the whole meal, then it is "his" or "her" meal. You consume it, but you don't really own it. If you are invited over to Thanksgiving and the host asks you to bring a dish to pass, then the meal changes. The meal is now "our" meal. And you are super excited to ask what others think about your cheesy potatoes.

If right now you look at the church and say, this is what "they" do versus this is what "we" do, I have a hunch you're not involved.

Yet, our society sets us up to be savvy consumers. In every other environment, we are judging spaces, products, and people. And we are good at picking out the best. Savvy consumerism is what is behind some of the growth of mega-churches. (My theory anyway). Like Chipotle has perfected the burrito, so mega-churches have perfected church. The spaces, people, and product of the mega-churches are done well, and so it's attractive. But unfortunately, much of the growth has to do with consumeristic Christians versus contributors.

Consumeristic Christianity is proved by statistics. In 2022, it was reported by Gallup that 35% of people volunteered for a religious organization. This doesn't report the type of volunteering or frequency. This report simply records if volunteering happened at all. Volunteering was down from 44% in 2017.[19] A statement made by many in the church post-COVID is that people came back, but volunteers did not. The statistics seem to support that sentiment.

Where are you at? Like many topics in this chapter, we see again how much we wrestle with our sinful nature. We often want to make church about us, our preferences, and our comfortability. We want to be served and not have to serve.

Hallelujah for our Savior, Jesus. The One who did not come to be served, but to serve and give His life as a ransom for all. Hallelujah for forgiveness over our sin. Hallelujah for a new day and a fresh start to try to please God out of thanks for what He has done. Hallelujah for the Holy Spirit who empowers any good deed. And Hallelujah that there have been many faithful contributors in God's kingdom.

Amazing Love has had some incredible contributors. I look at our congregation and I've seen each family contribute in some form. I also look back at a track record of right hand people. People who were so generous, so dedicated, and so giving that it brought life and opportunity to our church. I think of a young couple hosting our Core Group meetings and holding fellowship meals to get to know others. I think of fellow church planters who breathed encouragement and hope into my ministry for the Lord and saw in me what I couldn't see in myself. I think of staff members and their families who go above and beyond in so many ways that the world will never see, but angels rejoice over. I think of the generous business men and women who worked so hard in the world in order to support our Gospel ministry and make it easy for many more to see Jesus.

Don't ever underestimate the impact you can make as you decide to be a contributor at your local church. I'm ever inspired by this quote from D.L. Moody, "The world has yet to see what God can do with a man fully consecrated to him. By God's help, I aim to be that man."[20] Will you aim to be that man or woman? Where can you continue to grow?

But as you make that choice to serve as God served you, let me give you what I have learned to be the secret to sustained passion and service to the Lord.

It was Amazing Love's two-year anniversary. We went all out in our community to make an impact for Jesus and to reach as many as possible. We sent out fifteen thousand invitational postcards. I had handwritten and personally delivered over twenty invitations to community members who were interested in our church. We planned an incredible sermon series on Elijah to be kicked off on that day. I invited our best musicians, a band called Koiné, to join us for the Sunday. And to top it off we had free Aurelio's pizza lunch for any and all – some of the finest pizza in all Chicagoland.

On my way over to church, I got teary eyed in eager anticipation. I was so excited and passionate! I had said so many prayers about potential guests that I thought this would be Pentecost 2.0. Three thousand might come to know Jesus today! God did it once, why wouldn't he do it again? Realistically, I thought even if we have just a couple new guests to share the Gospel with, it would be great!

It was a great day. The Gospel was shared, Koiné was awesome, and the pizza was good. But do you want to guess how many guests showed up? 0. Zero. None. Nada.

I remember hearing a similar story shared at seminary by my good friend, Pastor Ben Kuerth. He talked about going all out for a Sunday, and after all the work, they only had one guest. But the point he made was that angels still rejoice over one sinner who turns, and so he should rejoice over one.

I remember thinking about that story and my experience. With my full-on pouty spirit, I remember exclaiming in my heart, "Angels don't rejoice over zero!"

On my way back from church that day I was teary eyed for a different reason. I was disappointed. I was upset. I was confused about what God wanted. I remember having a conversation with my Heavenly Father. I was like, "You want this too right? You said the harvest is plentiful and the workers are few. I was in the harvest. I'm not perfect, but I just want them to see your Son!"

I didn't hear an audible voice from heaven. But I do imagine what my Heavenly Father would have said. It went something like this. "Son, what are you doing all this for? Are you doing all this work for My kingdom, for results and what you can see? Because I have to tell you, before you ever arrived on the scene, My kingdom was just fine. I know those who are Mine. I'm in control of that. But if you are doing this because you love Me, that's all I wanted."

From that day on, I learned that the only true motivation I have for sustained service, passion, and all out activity for God's kingdom is this: I get to love God and give Him my heart. **My business is to love God from the heart with all that I do and all that I am, and His business is to do whatever He wants with that.**

Perhaps you stopped serving or giving because you didn't see the results you wanted. Perhaps along the way, you believed the devil's lie that it was all in vain, and you were wasting your time. Please don't make service to Jesus about you and your expectations. It's really not about you.

It's about loving and praising the Rock who is so much higher than us all. The One worthy of all our praise. The King of kings and Lord of lords! The One whose paths are beyond tracing out and whose ways are higher than our ways.[21]

And He reminds us of one very important thing. When we lose ourselves in service to Him - it will never (regardless of results), it will never (regardless of the approval of others), it will never (regardless of what history makes of it), **never be in vain.**

Hear this beautiful truth, "Therefore, my dear brothers and sisters, stand firm. Let nothing move you. Always give yourselves fully to the work of the Lord, because you know that your labor in the Lord is not in vain" (1 Corinthians 15:58).

Let's make church about Jesus, not about me.

STUDY QUESTIONS

1) Think on a time you stepped out in faith following God's clear command. How did things turn out? In what ways does God call us to get comfortable being uncomfortable?

2) What are the two tenets of the Great Commission? Why are they both so important? How are they currently accomplished at your church home?

3) What are your preferences when it comes to the church, especially worship? What is your favorite worship song? What are the essentials in worship? What are simply traditions in your church?

4) Does your church do anything that makes it difficult for unbelievers to turn to God? If so, what changes could be made? Is that change an area of Christian freedom or not?

5) Have you ever gone through motions of worship? What part of worship is it particularly easy to clock out of? What styles or personalities are most distracting to you in worship? How can you work to overcome it?

6) Are you currently more of a consumer or a contributor at church? In what ways have you been or are involved? What are opportunities to increase your involvement in your church?

IDENTITY

Identity theft is real.

A few years back I saw an interesting charge on my credit card statement. It was for a flight to Bangkok. While I love to travel, and would definitely love to visit Thailand, I had not planned this trip. Apparently, the one who booked it was Demitri Rostraustiovich. As cool as that name sounded, it was not me. I am and always will be Dustin Steven Blumer. Thankfully, working with my credit card company, I was able to recover the money spent on that flight, and perhaps one day Dustin, not Demitri, will book a flight to Bangkok. It wasn't the only time my identity was stolen. Another time someone impersonating me via email said I was stuck in London and needed money quickly. Thankfully a generous friend, who was about to open his wallet and get me unstuck, let me know about it.

In 2022, there were more than 40 million cases of identity theft in the U.S., resulting in 43 billion in losses.[1]

Yet, identity theft isn't just a financial issue, it is a very real spiritual issue. And the enemies trying to steal our identity are three-fold.

Satan, a.k.a. the accuser, is trying to steal our identity. He uses "un" words to do so. He says we are unlovable, unacceptable, unremarkable, unredeemable, and unforgivable. The people in the world around us are attempting to steal our identity. They foist hurtful ideas upon us giving the impression it is the new normal. People of the world use the idea of "us" to redefine who we are. They say, "you're crazy like us, you're dirty like us, you're a lost cause like us, you're an addict like us." The last enemy steal our identity is fairly surprising. It's our own ideas of who we are. I don't know about you, but the worst things I've ever heard said about me...came from me.

Have you ever been on a quest to find out who you really are? Perhaps, you've taken personality tests. I know I have. I've completed my DiSC profile. In Meyers Briggs I am an ESTJ which changed from the last time I took the test. In StrengthsFinder, my top 5 Strengths are 1) Includer, 2) Activator, 3) Connectedness, 4) Achiever, 5) Belief. And finally my Enneagram is type 1, the Reformer. Yet, the reality is I am still on a quest to figure out who I am on any given day.

As people, we change houses, change jobs, change relationships, change preferences based on who we think we are, and who we want to become.

But the reality is that we are often wrong about who we say we are. Consider what the prophet Jeremiah said about the nature of our innermost thoughts and feelings. He said, "The heart is deceitful above all things and beyond cure. Who can understand it" (17:9). What Jeremiah is telling us is that we lie to ourselves about ourselves.

In the United States, one of the idols we have been pursuing is the idea of our authentic self. Marriage is no longer an opportunity to give God glory by serving a spouse and kids - it's an opportunity to pursue oneself and one's vision board. Jobs no longer have to provide for the family alone, they need to fill the cup of self-fulfillment and purpose. Even one's own gender is in question if the feeling of the authentic self is not there.

Want a solution to identity theft? **Better than your idea of you is God's idea of you.** Better than letting Satan, the world, or even ourselves define us is allowing God to define us. It is then that our true identity will never be, and can never be stolen. It is then that true peace and joy can be had. It is then that clear direction will come, regardless of cultural norms, internal feelings, or Satan's temptations.

So what does God say about us?

1) You are a child of God

"See what great love the Father has lavished on us, that we should be called children of God! And that is what we are" (1 John 3:1).

My good friend Pastor Jeff Gunn was a missionary in Africa for fifteen years. In many ways he was living the dream of anyone caught up with the Great Commission! He lived out in the bush of Zambia and went to various churches around Africa preaching the Gospel. But, after fifteen years, he decided to serve the Lord as a high school teacher in his hometown of Phoenix, Arizona. Upon taking the new position as a high school teacher he experienced a major bout with clinical depression. He couldn't get out of bed or function normally. He sought counseling and discovered something that would change his life and help him overcome. The counselor was able to point out that the majority, if not all of his identity, was wrapped up in being a missionary in Africa. And if he was no longer that, who was he? The way forward was understanding his most important identity. While he was no longer a missionary in Africa, he was still a child of God. This was the identity, and the Gospel promise that set him free from depression.

Child of God is our most secure identity.

Consider your other identities as student, boss, employee, boyfriend, spouse, son, daughter, mother or father. All of these identities are subject to failure and dissolution. What happens when the whole of your identity is as mother and you forgot to pick up your kids? What happens when your identity is as spouse and you get divorced? What happens when your identity is as straight A student and you fail the test? The answer is that it can leave us hurting and less than. If I am no longer a perfect mom, a spouse, a straight A student, than what am I?

You are a child of God. This identity was won for you not by your performance, but by the performance of Jesus on the cross. He made a way for sinners to be called the sons and daughters of the most high God by the blood that He shed. And no one can take that identity from you. If you are in faith, you are in the family, and no one is kicking you out. If you are in faith, you stand in grace, and the merits of Christ cover the sins of this day.[2] Because this identity is based on the performance of Jesus and not our own, we cannot fail at it. Child of God is simply who we are.

As a child of God we have a Father who loves us more than we know.

Do you know what galaxy we live in? If you answered the Milky Way you not only know about candy bars, but you also know about astronomy. I want you to consider the vastness of this galaxy. Imagine you found a penny somewhere in the contiguous United States - from New York to California. A penny found in the United States, is the same scale as our solar system in our Milky Way galaxy.[3] That is how big this galaxy is, and we struggle sending satellites past Mars. Do you know how many galaxies there are? Scientists would say billions, but they are limited based on how far telescopes can see.

God says to his children, "For as high as the heavens are above the earth, so great is his love for those who fear him" (Psalm 103:11). The heavens, or the galaxies, go far beyond our understanding. Therefore, I believe God is saying, "You have no idea how much I love you. It goes way beyond what you can possible know!"

And our Father's love is seen in how He protects His children in any circumstance, and knows how to give good things in any condition.

There is a story in the Bible I come back to again and again. It's the story of Hagar. If you don't know it, I encourage you to open to Genesis 16. Abraham and Sarah were promised a child, but it wasn't coming according to their timeline. Sarah had the idea that her husband would sleep with her maidservant Hagar, and perhaps that is how God's promise would come true. (By the way, if you need to sin to accomplish God's will, I'm pretty sure it's not God's will). Abraham didn't come up with the idea, but he didn't fight it either. And what could Hagar do or say?

So Abraham slept with Hagar and it worked…I guess. Hagar became pregnant and bore a son named Ishmael. But no, I take it back, it didn't work, because Sarah became jealous and cruel to Hagar. So cruel that Hagar was forced out of the household, and left to fend for herself. Shortly after she ran away, an angel of God appeared to her, and promised that she and her child would be blessed. Hagar reflected upon this and said of God, "You are the God who sees me" (16:13).

God took care of Hagar when no one else did, and why? Because as a child of God, Hagar was loved more than she possibly knew.

So are you!

2) You are a foreigner

One of my favorite things to do is to travel and stay in new hotels. Because I'm usually on vacation when I do this, I splurge a little bit. You know the softness of a fresh towel? I like to experience that over the very used, old, and not-always-so-soft towels of the hotel. So I go out and purchase a couple of new towels. But it doesn't stop there. I am a stickler for a good pillow - it needs to be the exact right height for my neck - so while I'm out getting towels, I pick up a pillow or two as well. One stay I just did NOT agree with the design, particularly the pictures of cornfields on the walls. So…I had to pick up a new picture to change the ambiance of the room. Finally, once I stayed while the Final Four was on, and I couldn't bear the tiny hotel room tv. So…you guessed it, I went to Best Buy and got a much larger, clearer TV in order to watch the games.

At this point you, might be thinking, "Did you really do this? What are you thinking changing the art and the TV? I can possibly understand towels, but I mean you're only there for a night or a couple of days."

And if you thought that…I have you right where I want you. I don't do any of that. I just wanted to point out how ridiculous it would be to custom make a hotel room that you don't stay in for long. It's not home, so it's ridiculous to treat it that way.

Right now, wherever you live, however long you've lived there, it's just a hotel room. You are not home, and a time is coming sooner than you know when you will leave and finally go home.

The Apostle Peter pointed this out when he wrote, "Live out your time as **foreigners** here in reverent fear" (1 Peter 1:7).

And if that premise is true there are certain implications on how we should live right now.

If we are foreigners, then whether this season of life is the best or the worst, it will all soon fade.

We understand this from vacations. Sometimes you get to the end of a vacation, and you are dreading the last day because you know it will soon be over. You cannot stay in Hawaii forever - you indeed have to go home and get back to work. Sometimes you get to the end of vacation and can't wait to go home because the vacation was awful. (Like this one time in Mexico, where the resort didn't have proper A/C, and after five days in constant sweat, our favorite part was getting back to the airport with temperature control). Good or bad, both soon fade when you're on vacation.

I consider this through the lens of the Parable of the Rich Man and Poor Lazarus. There is a picture of their earthly lives. Here's a picture of the rich man, "There was a rich man who was dressed in purple and fine linen and **lived in luxury every day**"(Luke 16:19). He was living the dream, every day, but it did not matter. Then we come to Lazarus who is known by name, some say that is because God knows him and all believers by name. We hear about his earthly conditions, and that he was, "covered with sores and longing to eat what fell from the rich man's table. Even the dogs came and licked his sores" (Luke 16:20-21). And even though it was tough for Lazarus, every day, it did not matter.

123

What mattered was their home, not their hotel. Lazarus we read went to his eternal home with the Lord. For all eternity, he enjoyed joys that never end. The rich man was separated from God at home in hell. For all eternity, he suffered misery that would never end.

This parable is a good reminder not to lose your home in heaven for the pursuit of a comfy hotel here on earth. This parable is also a reminder for a believer who is suffering that this pain is both light and momentary. This parable ultimately is a comfort to believers and a warning for unbelievers. **For believers, this earth is as bad as it will get, and it only gets better. For unbelievers, this earth is as good as it will get, and it will only get worse.**

I wonder, have you ever felt like a foreigner? You didn't fit the culture, the ideas and language all seemed strange, and nothing hit quite right?

I remember a childhood dream come true when I was young. We were able to go to the happiest place on earth, Disneyland in California. We rode the tea cups, met Mickey, and saw Cinderella's castle. What could be better than a kid having a day in Disneyland? Yet, even this most incredible day was far from perfect. My sister spilled my dad's hot coffee all over me, and my mom was terrified by the new Star Wars ride.

Even our best days in this foreign land will never be perfect. You can do all you wanted on the weekend, buy the newest technology and latest fashion, see incredible sights, and still be left wanting. **No matter how much we pursue heaven on earth, this earth will never be heaven.**

I love how C.S. Lewis put it, "If we find ourselves with a desire that nothing in this world can satisfy, the most probable explanation is that we were made for another world."[4] If you have found even on your best days, that it didn't scratch the itch, then perhaps it just reminds us we are not yet home. Yes, you and I are foreigners.

3) You are a royal priest.

> "But you are a chosen people, a royal priesthood, a holy nation, God's special possession, that you may declare the praises of him who called you out of darkness into his wonderful light" (1 Peter 2:9).

It's not just a pastor's job to tell people about the love of Jesus. It's the job of every Christian - you are a royal priest! Yet, studies show that not everyone believes this. In 1993, 10% of Christians believed it was not their job to share the faith - today that percent is 30%.[5] A study by Lifeway Research found that out about three in ten unchurched Americans have never had someone share the faith with them.[6] And many Christians do not feel equipped to do this work.

Based on our identity as priests, we must do this work. We must seize the opportunities that are all around us.

The first thing to do is analyze who is in your mission field or your "FRAN" network. FRAN stands for Friends, Relatives, Associates, and Neighbors. The people in your FRAN network represent those who need to hear the love of Jesus through you. So consider...is there anyone right now in that network that doesn't know the love of Jesus? If so, who is it?

The next step in priesthood is to pray for that person. Ask that God might give you opportunities to share the faith, and ask that you might share the faith boldly and clearly. Ask that the Spirit might use the Word to do for them what God has done for you, bring them from darkness to light.

Finally, consider the various ways of sharing the faith. Do you have a good church home? Invite them to it and let your pastor share God's Word. Do they have any spiritual questions that represent obstacles for them? Seek the answer from Scripture through your own study or with the help of a pastor. Do they know you care for them? Often ears won't be open until they learn that you sincerely want what is best for them. On this point, I love this statement by President Theodore Roosevelt: "People don't care how much you know until they know how much you care."[7]

In today's culture, one of the easiest ways of sharing the faith is simply sharing your story. Share how God has worked in your life to call you from light to darkness, and what you love most about being a Christian.

For me, I look for opportunities to bring a conversation to my occupation. I ask them what they do for work, and many times they return the question. When I say I'm a pastor, I simply ask the question, "Do you have a church home?" The responses to that are telling and many times present an opportunity for me to share my story.

My story sounds like this, "I had Christian parents who baptized me as a baby, and while I've never been perfect, I've been a part of God's family all my life. I wanted to become a pastor because eternity far outweighs these mere moments on earth, and I didn't want to waste my life on less-than things. I love sharing Jesus with others because we all deal with guilt, shame, fear and anxiety, and Jesus has an answer for all those. In Jesus, I find my truest treasure, the one who loves me perfectly, and the one true constant of life." Many times I've found people are receptive to hearing a personal story regardless of their current beliefs or objections.

Yet, I will always still advocate for a clear Gospel presentation. Often the lead up question is, "Can I tell you what I believe?" From there I've relied on the Bridge (a simple picture illustration with six points). Those six points are pretty easy to memorize, and you don't have to be Da Vinci to get the drawing right. Simply draw two cliffs making a chasm and a cross that is the bridge between it. Those six life-changing, Biblical points are as follows:

1) The biggest problem is that sin separates us from God.
2) Sin leads to death in this life and in hell.
3) We can't get to God by our goodness.
4) God comes to us at Christmas.
5) Jesus lives for us, and dies for us.
6) The cross is the bridge to get to God.

Doing the work of a priest is what leads many, many more to join us in our heavenly home.

4) You are fearfully and wonderfully made.

"For you created my inmost being; you knit me together in my mother's womb. I praise you because I am fearfully and wonderfully made; your works are wonderful, I know that full well" (Psalm 139:13-14).

You were not behind the idea of you, God was behind the idea of you. And He got it right.

At one point or another, we all question how and why we were made. It could be a comparison to someone else we idolize that gets us to doubt who we are. It could be a trauma of the past that makes us uncomfortable in our own skin and looking for an escape. It could be what someone else has said we should or should not be.

Regardless of the reason, many Americans are wrestling with an identity crisis. There are surgeries for those who want to look like they do on their Snapchat filter. There are people who try to look like cartoon celebrities such as Jessica Rabbit from *Who Framed Roger Rabbit*.[8] Pronouns for people have expanded from he and she, to they and them. Gender neutral bathrooms have become common. Students go to school dressed as furries, feeling more comfortable to identify as an animal rather than a human being.

Then there are the ways we all try to cover up who we truly are whether through makeup, dressing up, or trying to fit in. We often want to be the opposite of how God made us as we envy what others have been given.

Yet, God provides a clear path forward. Trust Him for who He says you are, trust that what He made was made on purpose and not by accident. Trust that we do not have to remake what He put together. Trust that He has given you unique gifts and abilities because of your unique design.

I consider these compelling words from Isaiah,

> "Woe to those who quarrel with their Maker, those who are nothing but potsherds among the potsherds on the ground. Does the clay say to the potter, 'What are you making?' Does your work say, 'The potter has no hands'" (Isaiah 45:9).

Right now, are you quarreling with God about how He made you? Why you are not taller, thinner, with less acne, with more hair, more blonde hair, bigger eyes, blue eyes, more muscle, less fat, more intelligence, less body hair, etc. **For the rest of our lives, we could wrestle with all God didn't make us to be, or we could praise Him for all He did make us to be.** And what He made you to be is wonderful!

I consider Ford automobile company. I've always loved the Mustang, and in its many forms it is a beautiful car. But let's say one day the owner of a '67 Shelby Mustang decides it shouldn't be a car - it should be a boat. So he takes out all the raw materials and adds some new parts to try to turn it into a boat. He takes out the engine and puts propellers in the back. He tries to mold the shape and add some material to make it float. After years of work and investment the Mustang is finally seaworthy, but to be honest, it's not a great boat. Though, it would have always been a great car. (By the way, someone actually did this very thing).[9]

You will never be great at impersonating something or someone you weren't made to be. You will always be great when you accept who God, your Maker, says you are.

So we end with our beginning thought: **better than your idea of you is God's idea of you.**

But how can we accept this, more than that, *pursue* this in a world that pushes living for our own ideas of who we are? We'll have to say, "it's not about me." And we'll have to look again at our Savior, Jesus.

Consider this passage from Philippians.

> "Who, being in very nature God, did not consider equality with God something to be used to his own advantage; rather, he made himself nothing by taking the very nature of a servant, being made in human likeness" (Philippians 2:6-7).

From that passage, we see that Jesus gave up His true identity as God to become like us. He became fully human not for His own sake, but for ours. **He became what He was not, so we could be what we are not.**

If Jesus sacrificed His identity out of love for us, may we sacrifice our ideas of identity out of love for Him. May we accept what our Maker proclaimed, calling us "fearfully and wonderfully made." May we know that in Christ, the old has gone and the new has come. May we pursue a lifestyle that continually conforms to the likeness of Christ - regardless of what culture, our own feelings, or Satan says about it.

STUDY QUESTIONS

1) Have you ever taken a personality test? What did the results reveal? How kind or negative is your self-talk? Are there any other strong voices in your life that have the potential to shape your identity?

2) In what ways does our world reward good performance, and punish bad performance? Why is "child of God" such a solid identity? In what ways do you know God's love for you?

3) Do you recall a particularly good season of life? Can you recall sin still being in that season? Do you recall a particularly bad season of life? Can you recall God's grace still being in that season? Read Psalm 90:10-12. What wisdom is found in those verses?

4) Is there anyone in your "FRAN" network you can be praying for, and looking to share the Gospel with? Write down your faith story. What friend could benefit from hearing God's work in your life? Write down and memorize the steps of the Bridge.

5) What do you love about how God made you? What would you change if you could? How can you find contentment with who you are right now?

CONTROL

C oncerning ourselves with what we cannot control is one way to go crazy.

Calling all backseat drivers. Have you ever wanted to take the wheel from someone who wasn't going the correct speed, taking the fastest route, or driving how you would? It's a miserable way to spend a road trip, much better is to relinquish control or beg to drive. Calling all helicopter parents. Have you ever dropped your kid off and couldn't stop thinking about what they were up to? Much better is to recognize the same God who is with you is also with them. Calling all frugal financial managers. Have you ever freaked out by how someone else used the credit card, or thought the world was ending based on how little was in your bank account? Much better is to rely on the God who feeds birds and clothes flowers and calls you way more valuable.

If you can relate to any one of these examples, so can I for all three. But have you ever wondered what is behind our quest for control?

According to WebMD (which is super helpful and never leads anyone to believe they have cancer when they don't, ha!) what could be behind a desire for control is anxiety and the need for peace. "People with anxiety disorders feel a need to control everything around them in order to feel at peace. They may not trust anyone else to handle things the way they will."[1] That's one take, here's another, "By trying to exert control over every aspect of a situation, you may be trying to create a sense of security and predictability."[2]

The reasons behind a desire for control are multi-faceted. Yet, I believe what many see in a control freak is really someone who craves security and peace.

And what happens to control freaks when they are not in control? They freak out! There is no security or peace.

Reflect with me on COVID-19. COVID-19 led to many canceled plans. My wife and I had a trip to Paris and Iceland that would have been epic. Unfortunately, it never happened. COVID-19 led to fears about health, the threat, and the reality of death. We all wondered what it might do if we caught it, and some of us lost loved ones along the way. COVID-19 changed the workplace. Not only with the work from home movement, but also it started the Great Resignation.[3] Stores closed, employees left, and things haven't really been the same. COVID-19 changed our schools. Online schooling was the only option for months, or for longer. Everyone was forced to learn in front of a screen. COVID-19 changed church. In a positive way it forced many churches to share the Gospel online, and it flooded the internet with Gospel content. In a negative way it devastated large group gatherings in a way the church has yet to recover from.[4] COVID-19 changed the family. Family walks and dinners, game nights and collaborative dancing were at an all time highs! But perhaps the greatest thing COVID-19 did was teach us this simple truth: **we are not in control.**

And because we were not in control, it led to a mental health crisis. Record numbers of people dealing with anxiety in some form or fashion. The World Health Organization cited that anxiety and depression grew by 25%.[5]

But what if we approached control differently? What if we said about control, "it's not about me." **If we give up our quest for control, we can find true peace in the One who is in control.**

Consider the comfort found in this passage,

> "He **raised Christ from the dead** and seated him at his right hand in the heavenly realms, **far above** all rule and authority, power and dominion, and every name that is invoked, **not only in the present age but also in the one to come**. And God placed all things under his feet and appointed him to be **head over everything for the church**" (Ephesians 1:20-22).

I love that our God isn't just above all things. He is **far above**. This reminds me of the USA's first Dream Team with Jordan, Bird, Barkley, Ewings, and Johnson. The Dream Team wasn't just above every other team. They were **far above**. The games were over before they began, because no other competition stood close. On average they scored fifty-two more points than the other teams.[6]

Right now I want you to picture that. I don't know what feels over you. Is it the politics of this age, the company and boss you report to, the school whose academic hoops you are trying to jump through? God isn't just above all this, He is **far above**.

And it isn't just that He will be reigning and revealed as King of kings someday. **He is reigning right now!** Yes, the world is irrevocably broken. No, the world will not get better until Jesus obliterates this world and makes a new one. But it doesn't stop our Almighty God from reigning right now. Who but our Almighty God can take all things (even the most miserable moments) and work them for our good? What incredible authority that proves!

And now to my favorite point. Who is Jesus reigning for? Who is Jesus using His control for? **Jesus controls all things for us, His church.** He rules and reigns out of love for us. I believe He is orchestrating all things so that He will have a tighter grip on our hearts. He rules so that many more might know Him who is above all things. And He does it so that the peace and security we crave, we'll find in Him.

And if you want proof that our God is in control, God says consider the resurrection. Jesus was dead but is now raised to life. When many thought death was in control, or the devil had won, Jesus rose above them. As the One who conquered death, He declares that He and He alone is in control.

When I was growing up, our family vacations consisted of road trips - looong road trips. We'd drive through the night to Florida or Texas from Wisconsin. It gave me plenty of time to pump the jams of MC Hammer on my Walkman cassette player. It was the glorious age of conversion vans, where the back seat turned into a queen size bed. And whether we were driving through the Appalachian Mountains of Tennessee or the plains of Illinois, I had peace. I felt secure even when we took quick turns and stopped so abruptly I slid across that queen size bed. (Seatbelt laws were more lax then). You want to know why? Because I trusted the driver. In my mind, my dad was the greatest driver in the world, and nothing bad could happen with him at the wheel. So whether I was listening to cassettes or sleeping, I felt peace.

In life we are not the drivers, but the passengers. Our God who is at the wheel can be trusted, and that means we can have peace.

Let's talk about a few areas where for the sake of peace, we may need to relinquish control.

1) We are not in control of our plans

"We make plans, God laughs."

It's a phrase that many in my circles of public ministry toss around. There are pastors and teachers who have said in the past, "I would never do that! No way I would ever live there!" Guess what they are doing, and where they live now? You guessed, they are doing exactly what they said they would never do. They live in places they ruled out once before.

I had a very specific plan as third grader. I was going to be a pastor, never marry, and drive a neon orange 911 Porsche. My parents said that car is also where I would be living based on my salary. But as a kid, if I could drive a Porsche - that was a glad concession I was willing to make. I loved cars, didn't know much about girls, or the needs of an adult. God has allowed only one of those desires to come true, and I'm so thankful. Turns out having a bedroom and a bathroom are pretty great. Not only that, but my wife, Kat, is my greatest gift besides faith in Jesus. My two daughters taught me how far God's love must go, because I would do anything for them. They bring so much joy to this life - much more than a fast car.

I'm so glad God didn't take me up on my third grade ideas for life. **God's plans for me are so much better than my plans for me.**

Did you have any plans that you thank God He said no to? What grace is ours when God says no to our less-than plans for life!

Consider this promise of our loving God, "'For I know the plans I have for you,' declares the Lord, 'plans to prosper you and not to harm you, plans to give you hope and a future'" (Jeremiah 29:11). God's plans for you are so, so good.

God planned your birthday before your parents did (Psalm 139:15-16). God planned to pursue you with His mercy and goodness (Psalm 23:6). God planned where you'd live and how long you'd live in order for your pursuit of Him to take place (Acts 17:26). God planned to give you unique talents and abilities that you might have avenues to help others and give Him great glory (Ephesians 2:10). God planned to redeem evil, misfortune, and bad days for your good and for the refining of your faith (Romans 8:28, 1 Peter 1:6-7). God planned on providing forgiveness for any misstep along life's way (1 John 4:10). God planned that regardless of your family circumstances or circle of friends you would know perfect love (Psalm 36:7). God planned that you would be with Him in heaven someday (John 14:3).

Do you think the same God could be trusted for the plans of this day, or for this season of life? But how do we get there?

The Lord's Prayer is not only the Master's class on prayer, it is also Jesus' teaching to live a life that's - you guessed it - "not about me." Of the seven petitions or requests, only one has to do with our earthly needs. The other six petitions have to do with God and spiritual concerns. If you pray this over and over, you will be asking of God, "Your will be done." And when we seek God's will fervently, we can more easily accept if He has a different plan for our day or our lives.

"Your will be done" is behind one of God's greatest commands. Jesus said, "For whoever wants to save their life will lose it, but whoever loses their life for me will find it" (Matthew 16:25). If we do not constantly set our sights higher than ourselves, we have the potential to lose our lives eternally. If we set our sights higher than ourselves and onto the will of God, we have the potential not only to gain heaven but also to make a difference on earth. About this idea C.S. Lewis said, "**Aim at heaven and you will get earth thrown in. Aim at earth and you get neither.**"[7]

Let's consider another reason to accept God's will above our own. It has to do with vision.

A scientist named Copernicus in the late 1500s had the idea that the earth is rotating around the sun.[8] He used geometrical diagrams to propose his theory, which upended the prevailing idea that the sun rotates around the earth. In the 1600s, Galileo came along with his telescope, with which he was able to see various phases of the planet Venus. His view of Venus in those phases, similar to the phases of the moon, lent support to Copernicus' idea that the earth rotates around the sun.[9] As telescopes grew in power, more and more was learned about the universe. The Hubble Telescope launched in 1990 led to even more discoveries. It has shown us the vastness of our universe filled with galaxies, and it has been used to prove the existence of black holes. [10] With greater vision came greater wisdom.

Why do I bring this up? Because you and I have tiny telescopes, and God has a bigger one. He sees everything - the past, the present, and the future with 20/20 vision. This makes Him wiser than we'll ever be. Because of His vision, we should relinquish our control for our way and our plans, and trust in His.

Perhaps this is why His ways are higher than our ways, and His thoughts higher than our thoughts.[11] Because His vision has always been higher as well.

Consider a home purchase. When the appraisal comes through, even if it was done correctly, do they know what's going to happen to the housing market in five years? When the home inspection is done, even if it is thorough, do they know if a natural disaster will destroy it? When the bank approves the loan, do they know if the company you currently work for will still be your place of employment for the length of the loan? Of course not! They all have a limited view, and so do we.

But God doesn't - He sees everything. So a good prayer for a home purchase is not, "God I really want it, please let it be." Instead, "God, it seems from my view to be good, yet Your will be done, because You see it all."

This isn't just true for houses. It's true for how we spend money, pursuits like a vacation or retirement, prayers over career change or school change, and our desires for our kids. An understanding of God's greater vision should make us crave to pray as Jesus taught, "Your will be done."

"So should I never plan? Are vision boards a bad idea? What if by nature, I am a planner?" Our plans aren't bad. Calendars are good, even necessary. Vision boards can be great exercises. There is a balance to teaching, and that balance has to do with the attitude towards our plans. Consider these words of James.

> "Now listen, you who say, 'Today or tomorrow we will go to this or that city, spend a year there, carry on business and make money.' Why, you do not even know what will happen tomorrow. What is your life? You are a mist that appears for a little while and then vanishes. Instead, you ought to say, 'If it is the Lord's will, we will live and do this or that'" (James 4:13-15).

James wasn't against calendars and vision boards. The issue James was pointing out was an attitude of arrogance about our plans in the face of God's authority. We should not hold onto the idea that we are in control. We must submit to the One who is in control. Which means we should make plans but be flexible. Pursue great activities as long as our hearts are open to God's greater plan. We should set out each day and each season with a plan, yet with the understanding that things may change because God might have a better plan for that day or season.

When we trust that God's plans for us are good, and we are open to God's big or small change of plan, we can find peace no matter how life may change. May God grant such peace.

2) We are not in control of other people

There is only one person you are in control of, and that is only half the time and with the help of the Holy Spirit. Do you know who that is? Yourself.

All other people are either inside our sphere of influence or outside our sphere completely. So what happens to us when we try to control the actions of other people? We go crazy.

People will come into our lives and go out of our lives in ways that we can't control.

This past year I had a seminary classmate called to heaven because of a reckless driver. His name was Aaron Strong, and he left behind a beautiful family: his wife, Abbie, and two children, Hannah and Elijah. I saw God use Abbie's confessions of faith in incredible ways. On the day he was taken to heaven, she confessed, "He was the best dad, friend and pastor. God is good all the time. HE has this all figured out and will get us through the days to come. Lord, help me!"[12] I marvel at that confession in those circumstances. She calls out God's control of all things, reminding us, "HE has this all figured out." I've had a chance to talk with Abbie since, and she hasn't stopped proclaiming God's goodness. Abbie didn't know the day her husband would be called to heaven.

Neither do we. We don't know how long we'll have with family or friends. These people represent the gifts God gave us, but they were not promised to be in our earthly lives forever.

Yet, when people come and go, God will remain. Consider the names we have for God. He is the Alpha and Omega - which are the first and last letters of the Greek alphabet. He is from everlasting to everlasting. It's mind-boggling that God didn't have a birthday. He is the Great "I AM." He just exists now, in the past, and forever. If we are looking for the security of someone who will always be there, it is not with any one person, but with our God.

People will fail us, and we can't control it.

"The student is not above the teacher, nor a servant above his master. It is enough for students to be like their teachers, and servants like their masters. If the head of the house has been called Beelzebul, how much more the members of his household" (Matthew 10:24-25).

Jesus warned His disciples before sending them out that they would face obstacles because of their service to God.

Consider Jesus' own disciples. Most of them were confused half the time by what He said. In His hour of need, they all deserted Him. One denied knowing Him after confessing he would die with Him. And one backstabbed Him in such a memorable way that the name for all backstabbers nowadays is Judas.

If you follow Jesus, I think it is fair to say many won't understand why you follow Him and what you are up to as a Christian. Those nearest to you may desert you in your hour of need, some may deny you, and friends may backstab you. All of which you can't control. People are fickle, and even the best people on their best days will get it wrong.

A solution for this problem is living for the One who cannot fail us. Live for the One who is constantly good and faithful. Live for an audience of One. The only approval that will matter for all eternity is the approval and opinion of God. The one we are to seek to please above all others is our God.

I love how Paul put it, "Am I now trying to win the approval of human beings, or of God? Or am I trying to please people? If I were still trying to please people, I would not be a servant of Christ" (Galatians 1:10).

Consider if we spent most of our time trying to gain the approval of people who are here today and gone tomorrow? What a waste of time and energy! What a way to go crazy!

Again, there is a balance here. I'm not saying you shouldn't love people or serve them. God makes it very clear to love people, seek peace and unity, and even please them if it is possible. I'm also not saying people will always let us down. Many love us in ways far better than we've loved them. What I am saying is that regardless of how you love people, you will never be in control of their response. Some may surprise you in good ways, and some may not.

Let us find our peace in the faithfulness of God, not the fickle nature of people.

3) We are not in control of politics

One of my favorite stories in the whole of the Bible is Isaiah's prophesy of Cyrus.

> "This is what the Lord says to his anointed, to Cyrus, whose right hand I take hold of to subdue nations before him and to strip kings of their armor, to open doors before him so that gates will not be shut" (Isaiah 45:1).

You may ask, "That's a random favorite story. What in the world do you like about it?"

Thanks for asking. I think it is incredible that Isaiah is making a prophesy about Cyrus, calling him by name, over one hundred and fifty years before Cyrus was born! I think it is incredible that Cyrus, who was an awful tyrant of a ruler, could be used by God for God's own purposes. God would use King Cyrus and the nation of Babylon to punish His people for rebellion, mercifully calling them to repentance and reliance on Him. I think it is incredible how this account shows the control God has over earthly governments.

144

It's not the only time God did this. He flaunted His power in the face of Pharaoh through the 10 plagues, to call His people out of Egypt. The time set for them to be slaves in Egypt was determined by Him, and foretold to the exact year.[13] In the period of the Judges, He used other nations like a puppet-master, pulling the string every time His people need to be called back from their rebellion. Those that did not acknowledge His supremacy as King of kings He allowed to grow feathers and eat grass (such was the case for Nebuchadnezzar),[14] or die on the spot (such was the case for Herod the Great).[15]

God was and still is very much in control and above all earthly governments.

To understate it, America is divided by politics. Some like to say it's the worst it has ever been. While it's by no means ideal, I consider the Civil War and fellow citizens killing each other over various ideologies. I consider presidents who had lawsuits leveraged against them, shoes thrown at them, who were impeached, or shot and killed - and part of me thinks, "I'm not sure it's the worst it has ever been." And regardless of your opinion or my proof, politics is and always will be an emotional, contentious topic.

It seems with every new election, citizens of the United States say they will move to Canada, or that the world will end.

But if we believe the truths we just considered, then here is the comfort. Regardless of the newly elected politician, that person merely represents a puppet on God's string. Regardless of their good or evil intent, God knows how to use it for His purposes. Regardless of the earthly authority, God's power will still stand above it. Because it does, we can have comfort knowing He holds us in the palm of His hands.

Does this mean we should stop voting, stop lobbying, stop writing letters and appealing to our authorities? Does this mean we shouldn't pray or care? By no means! We should do all we can as citizens of this country to ensure America remains a great country. But after we did all we can do, we should trust in what God will do.

I love this quote by St. Augustine: "Pray as though everything depended on God. Work as though everything depended on you."[16] Do your part, but find rest in God.

Remember, He isn't just above all rule and authority, He is **far above** all rule and authority for us, His church.

Are you a control freak struggling to find peace and security?

Consider control and say, "it's not about me." Relinquish control to the One who has always had control. Let Him drive you through the ups and downs of life. For He isn't just the pathway to peace, Jesus is our peace.

STUDY QUESTIONS

1) Are there any areas of your life where you are tempted to be a control freak? What do you believe is behind that quest for control?

2) Read again Ephesians 1:20-22. What are the most comforting thoughts from those verses?

3) Do you remember any firm plans from younger years that did not turn out? In what ways has God blessed what was not in your plan?

4) How often do you end a prayer or request with "your will be done?" What have you found to be the balance between making plans and making room for God's plan?

5) Read Matthew 10:24-25. In what ways have you been treated like Jesus? Were you surprised when it happened? What does it look like for you to live for an audience of One?

6) What would you like to change about our country right now? Do you wish you had more control over our government? What can we do? How does the story of Cyrus give us peace?

CHILDREN

In the movie "The Grinch Who Stole Christmas," there is a pivotal scene. The Grinch's heart grew three sizes. Even after the Grinch stole their presents, after seeing the joy and gladness of the Whos in Who-ville on Christmas - his heart grew. His heart could no longer be measured, and it led him to return the presents and celebrate Christmas with the Whos.

Similarly, my heart grew when my daughters were born. Their birthdays were two of the greatest days of my life. I'm not sure my heart grew three sizes, but it was surely beating out of my chest. I didn't know I could love this deep, and that my heart had room to love each child so much.

Parents, can you relate to this? You don't have to grow up being a "kid person." You didn't have to birth them on your timeline or according to your vision board. Yet, if God so grants, a child can grow your heart in ways you can't even imagine. You become a "kid person." Parenting is a journey of love that lasts a lifetime, flowing from a heart that grew immeasurably.

Children represent one of the greatest gifts God can give. The Bible calls them a reward.[1] This doesn't mean children are God's plan for every couple or person. Remember children are God's idea before they become ours.[2] He knows how to bless families with children and without in unique ways. Yet, if you're on the fence about the idea, may the Spirit give you eyes to see them for the prize they are.

But children being one of the greatest gifts of God is part of our cultural problem. As with any great gift of God, such as a career, a spouse, or a prized possession, they can quickly become an idol. They can sit over the place of God in our hearts, and we can pursue them more than we pursue God.

Paul reminds us when it comes to worship, we have two options. We either worship the Creator above all things, or we worship created things. "They exchanged the truth about God for a lie, and **worshiped and served created things rather than the Creator**—who is forever praised. Amen" (Romans 1:25).

In Timothy Keller's book "Counterfeit Gods" he describes a counterfeit god this way. "A counterfeit god is something so central and essential to your life that, should you lose it, your life would hardly feel worth living."[3] The test to figure out your counterfeit god is this: "What has the potential to make you uncontrollably angry, anxious, or despondent if lost?"

The answer for many and thus the potential counterfeit god? Children. In fact, the worship of children represents one of the greatest forms of idolatry in America.

Ordered love is such an important concept for a Christian. We know we should love our children, our spouse, and we could even love our career for the matter. Love for our children is often an extension of our love for God, and a wonderful avenue to display selflessness. But that love needs to be in order, or life becomes out of whack. The ordered love our hearts should be pursuing is clear if you're married with children. Here is the ordered love: 1) God, 2) Spouse, 3) Children, and 4) Career. We understand number 1 pretty easily. Number 2 is clear because when we love our spouse, we are loving our children by creating a stable home. The lack of love between spouses tears at the security necessary for a child's development. Number 4 is also clear when it comes to our station of life. You may have many different careers and job titles, but your most unique station of life is as husband or wife, and as father or mother. To mix up any one of these is to commit idolatry, and it will have ramifications.

Here are some indications your love may be out of order. Do the desires of your children drive your pursuits with greater intensity than the desires of God? Does doing what makes your children happy more important than doing what makes God happy? Does God get the best of your time, talent, attention, and treasure, or do your children?

The honest reality is that our love is often out of order. The sin against the first commandment, "You shall have no other gods" is the sin that leads us to break all the others. To love God with all our heart, and with all our soul, and with all our mind, and with all our strength is the greatest and hardest command.

Thank God He loved us first and best. His love for us isn't dependent on how well we love Him back. Praise God the cross of Jesus covers the sin of idolatry. Praise God the Holy Spirit can empower us to live new lives according to His will. For repentant believers, our God has tossed this sin also into the depths of the sea and sees it no more.

But I had to start here. **Because children are so very close to our hearts, it's easy to make children "all about me."** Children become an extension of self-pursuit if we are not careful. So let's talk about three areas with children we need to declare, "it's not about me."

1) Healthy discipline requires an attitude that says, "it's not about me."

Disciplining children is not fun. If you want to have a good time, don't do it. Imagine you're taking the kids to Dairy Queen to get Blizzards and Dilly Bars. It's summertime and you want to have some fun and bond with the family. As you're packing into the minivan, your middle child hits the youngest child, and the youngest hits back. They don't know you saw it in the rearview mirror, but you did. You now have a choice. You could discipline them, or you could let it go. You choose discipline. You use a stern voice describing what you saw, and you give consequences. The middle child is now pouting and mad at you (somehow thinking you are the villain in this scenario), and the youngest child is crying. Talk about a mood-killer for what should have been a fun trip for ice cream.

Your inner dialogue goes something like this, "Don't they know why I chose to take them to DQ!? I could have just gone by myself, but I wanted them to have fun. I wanted to make some good memories. I wanted them to know I love them. Now neither of them feels like I love them, no one is happy, and I'm not even hungry anymore. Ahh!"

Perhaps this is why some parents used the familiar tagline for their discipline, "This is going to hurt me more than it hurts you." And what you doubted as child, you now tip your hat to as an adult.

Choosing not to discipline is a choice that can be made if "it's all about me." You may avoid momentary mood-killers. You may even become a momentary friend to your child as you join them on their wavelength. But it's the wrong choice.

Consider this verse from Proverbs: "Whoever spares the rod **hates** their children, but the one who **loves** their children is careful to discipline them" (Proverbs 13:24).

What is clear from this passage is that discipline is love. When you choose to forgo Dilly Bars to teach children they should not hit each other - that is love. When you see sinful attitudes, behaviors, and actions and attempt to course correct it - it is love, love, love. Make no mistake about it, and change your mainframe if need be, **discipline is love.**

Beyond that, Christian parents are not just armed with the law of God, but they also have opportunities than to point their children to the forgiveness of God. Discipline then becomes a parent's way to point their children to the cross of Jesus. What's more loving than that?

And what does the passage say about a lack of discipline? I find it interesting that Solomon doesn't just call it unwise, foolish, or simply not helpful. Through the inspiration of the Holy Spirit the word chosen for a lack of discipline is: hate. Hate, like how Joseph was viewed by his brothers who almost killed him. Hate, like how Amnon felt about Tamar after he disgraced her. Hate, like how Absalom, Tamar's brother, felt about Amnon and finally killed him. The same Hebrew word for hate is used in those accounts as it is here.[4] God is saying it is not love, kindness, or patience, but hate we have for our children if we do not discipline them.

Consider a child who is careless about crossing the road. They never look both ways on a busy street, they linger in the middle of it, and have a total lack of respect for what might happen. If a child one day is careless and the parent does nothing to prevent them from seeing their error of their ways, what could it lead to? Something worse for sure. If a parent would not discipline in this scenario we can see a lack of love.

In general I believe in using the lightest form of discipline that is effective, always combined with the forgiveness of God. Discipline without the understanding that one could be forgiven is more cruel than a lack of discipline in the first place. Discipline should clearly communicate, "Out of love for you, you cannot continue on this path."

One of the greatest things my parents did for me growing up was circling back after they disciplined me. They would explain why they did it, and how they loved me. Almost every time I knew I was wrong in the first place. I was able to see how hard it was for them to see me cry, or not get my way. They didn't enjoy it.

I reflect now on the love behind that discipline.

2) We must approach a child's success or failure with an attitude that says, "it's not about me."

Every child has a moment or season of rebellion. It doesn't always mean a parent did the wrong thing, and now a child is acting out. It's simply a reminder that we are not always in control. If parents take credit for either every failure or every success, it will lead to problems.

Bella, our firstborn, was colicky for her first three months of life. We had read "What To Expect When You're Expecting," and we were excited to raise our first child. But nothing could have prepared us for this. Well-intentioned parents gave us well-intentioned advice. However, everything they said we had already tried seven times. You try a lot of things during a whole night of screaming. We fed, burped, changed, rocked, drove, swung, played, and danced. For a few moments, if I ballroom danced to Josh Groban, the screaming would subside, but not for long. Parents would tell us how they interpret their children's crying, and that we should as well. With a full on spirit of snark, I wanted to record the consistent, unchanged loud screaming and quiz them to see if they'd noticed a difference. Instead, I nodded politely. Our first lesson as parents with a colicky baby was this: **no matter what we tried, sometimes we were not in control of our child's behavior.**

I saw it before as camp counselor and a pastor. Really good parents who did really right things had children with really wrong behavior.

Thankfully, I've been able to observe changing seasons. In general, love and discipline work in the long run, even if the current season is a hard one. Bella, who I thought must have hated us as a three-month-old infant is an awesome, friendly, smiley kid. The screaming stopped. Other kids I remember as unruly toddlers or campers are really kind, respectful young adults. Children go through all sorts of phases while they're growing up. And parents are often not in control.

We as parents do have great influence. We should do our best with what is in our sphere to teach them right and wrong, as mentioned with love and discipline. We should seek counsel and advice when we haven't come to a solution. But we shouldn't take in all the blame if at the end of the day a child rebels. If we do, we will have a lack of peace, and may even consider ourselves failures.

A great Biblical example is that of Job. He led by example for his family, and I'm sure shared God's truths regularly. He surely did with his wife on the worst day of his life.[5] At the beginning of Job's story it says,

"When a period of feasting had run its course, Job would make arrangements for them to be purified. Early in the morning he would sacrifice a burnt offering for each of them, thinking, 'Perhaps my children have sinned and cursed God in their hearts.' This was Job's regular custom" (Job 1:5).

He understood his children could rebel. Did he want them to? Of course not. As it said in the verse, he made arrangements for purification after feasting. This arrangement is built in accountability for his children, reminding them to stay pure. Would they always stay pure regardless of Job's intent? Job knew the answer, and so do we.

A child's rebellion isn't condemnation of the parent's influence - sometimes it's simply "not about me."

Similarly, a child's success isn't all up to the parent.

Again, parents do have great influence. I consider the story of Venus and Serena William's father. Richard Williams wanted to turn them into the tennis pros we know them to be today. It's reported that he had an eighty-five page written plan for them, and he started teaching them tennis at age four and a half. He coached his daughters for years. They combined to win one hundred twenty-two titles, thirty grand slams, and $175 million in prize money.[6] Influence does indeed matter.

But what happens if a parent thinks the child's success is all up to them, or is trying to live vicariously through their children? Similarly, it is not a good place to be, and it may skew priorities.

Parents who believe this might be convinced to overspend so their children can have an advantage. They might not want their children to fail, and so they help too much with homework. They may want their child to be a superstar athlete, dancer, or musician, believing that if they become a superstar, it means the family or the parent is a success.

Here I think of Joseph's story. His father, Jacob, led his household through favoritism that divided the family. It was a favoritism born out of polygamy and a favored wife. Joseph went on with remarkable morality and faith in God. He refused to sleep with Potiphar's wife, and he worked commendably in every position he held.[7] When interpreting Pharaoh's dream that would make him famous, he gave this confession about God, "'I cannot do it,' Joseph replied to Pharaoh, 'but God will give Pharaoh the answer he desires'" (Genesis 41:16). Joseph was a greater success than his father, Jacob, and in many ways saved his family. Why? Sometimes a child's success isn't about a parent's influence. Joseph was a success in spite of his father.

Why is this so important when it comes to parenting? Because peace is at stake one way or another. Peace is stolen through a child's failure, or peace is given through a child's success. Either way, if it's contingent on a child's performance, it's an unstable peace.

True peace and joy is found only in the constant nature of God and His unfailing love for us. He loves us regardless of how good or bad our parenting has been. He loves us regardless if our children look more like sinners or more like saints. He loves us regardless of what the world makes of us or our family members.

3) The most important responsibility of a parent that's "not about me" is a child's faith life.

Your greatest mission field is your immediate family. They need to hear of Jesus' love from you.

I love the story of Andrew, and what he did when he found Jesus. Recorded in John's account it says, "The first thing Andrew did was to find his brother Simon and tell him, "We have found the Messiah" (that is, the Christ)" (John 1:14). I'm glad Simon Peter found Jesus and became a believer, aren't you?

Sometimes there is a debate in parenting: if a parent should wait to let their children decide about religion when they are older. I understand the concern of parents whose true desire is for a child to want the faith versus having it force-fed. However, a child with a sinful nature does not know how to want Jesus until they are first shown His goodness.

Consider this Proverb: "Start children off on the way they should go, and even when they are old they will not turn from it" (Proverbs 22:6).

The influence of a parent sharing the faith at an early age is critical. It may even have eternal consequences. How good it is when parents pray for their children and have family devotion life. What a blessing to be able to talk about Jesus in the home, and answer any questions young ones may have. How awesome that God gave us in Baptism a washing of rebirth and renewal.[8] This way, from the very start, we can have confidence our children are not just part of our family - they are also part of God's family. What a lifelong blessing is instilled when children grow up with a habit of regular worship.

The impression parents give children about the faith is critical. If serving Jesus smacks more of a dreaded obligation than a joyful celebration, this will be picked up on by a child. If a different weekend opportunity is far more important and planned around than seeing Jesus, this silent sermon will be remembered.

The most important responsibility Christians parents have is to share Jesus with their kids.

And yet, the faith life of children is not up to the parents, it's not about them. First off, it is up to the Holy Spirit, who works through the Word and Sacraments to guide those children and rule their lives. As children grow up, their faith life will also be more and more up to them. As they grow into adulthood, they will have to choose if what was shared with them is what they want for the rest of their lives. They can continue to cooperate with the Holy Spirit, or they can rebel. Neither choice is up to the parents. The faith life of children is not about them.

It's no secret that the millennial generation has more and more people walking away from the faith. Well documented is the rise of the "nones" or those who claim no religious association.[9] The Christian faith will not be passed on to their children if they are not following. As noted, each millennial and each child rises and falls before their Savior alone.

But I do at times wonder what emphasis a current generation of parents is placing on faith in Jesus. Is there something the family seeks more than Him? Is there the sense of anticipation and joy when it comes to hearing from God? As with all things, there is forgiveness for any missteps. But let's do our best to teach our children the truth that there is no one greater than our God.

My hope is that this chapter grants guidance and peace to something we hold so dear, our children. My hope is that our children give us a window into the heart of God - that our love for our children can help us understand God's love for us. But may these great gifts never become walls blocking the love of God - may they not stand in the way of seeing Him and seeking Him with all our heart, all our strength, all our mind, and all our soul. God is our truest treasure and may He be our greatest love.

STUDY QUESTIONS

1) Do you remember the day your child was born? Read Psalm 103:13. In what ways does loving your child inform God's love for you?

2) In what ways do you see society idolizing children? Is it tempting for you to make your child an idol? Is there anything you can do differently to restore God's idea of ordered love?

3) Do you have a hard time discipling your child? Why or why not? In what ways have you emphasized forgiveness in your discipline? Would your children see the love behind your discipline right now? Why or why not?

4) Have you encountered a season of rebellion with your child? What did it look like? What is a promise of God that can help with that season?

5) What was one of your proudest moments as a parent? What does it look like to pursue God's glory in that moment as proud parent?

6) In what ways are you sharing Christ's love with your children? How important is passing on the faith to your family? Do your children see it as a family priority? In what ways can they see your prioritize the faith?

MARRIAGE

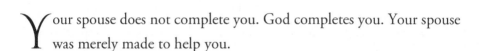

Your spouse does not complete you. God completes you. Your spouse was merely made to help you.

I want you to imagine that someone gave you an orange, and said that for the entire day, that orange was all you could eat. If that were the case, not only would you be completely unsatisfied and hungry, but you might try to squeeze out of the orange what it can't provide. You might go back to the slices to get every bit of fruit off of them. You might end up gnawing on the orange peel, even eating it. No matter what you do, an orange wasn't meant to satisfy your caloric needs for the day.

A three thousand calorie meal, consisting of a thirty-two ounce tomahawk steak, mashed potatoes, asparagus, dinner rolls, and chocolate mousse - now that's a different story. You could spread out those items during the day, or eat them all at once and be satisfied. Perhaps even be delighted.

God is the meal, and people are an orange. If we haven't filled up on God, we will try to squeeze out of another person something they weren't created to give. Like someone gnawing on an orange slice and left wanting, so it will be if we expect one person to meet all our needs. No person can, they weren't made to. But if we have already been filled up by an incredible meal, then we can treat an orange like an orange. An orange can be a great supplement along the way, but we're not going to die without it.

Marriage is an incredible blessing for those who enter into it. God said, "He who finds a wife finds what is good and receives favor from the Lord" (Proverbs 18:22). When God brought Adam together with Eve, He intended that this union we call marriage would be mutually beneficial. Solomon put it well saying, "Two are better than one, because they have a good return for their labor: If either of them falls down, one can help the other up. But pity anyone who falls and has no one to help them up" (Ecclesiastes 4:9-10). In marriage you have a teammate who will be with you - win, lose, or draw. In marriage you have the opportunity for children - a great reward from God. In marriage you can use the powerful gift of sex and be intimate with someone in a way you are not with anyone else. Marriage, simply put, rocks!

AND marriage is super hard. It's one of the most difficult arrangements on planet Earth. Live until death with the same person? Paul said, "Those who marry will face many troubles in this life" (1 Corinthians 7:28). Paul went on to describe how attention is divided as long as you are married. A married man or woman should rightly be concerned for his or her spouse. To complicate the matter, both man and woman are sinful by nature, and because of sin they are incompatible by nature. Differences between the sexes aren't always appreciated and celebrated, but mocked and ridiculed. The world offers escape routes constantly. Find your soulmate somewhere else? The world prompts us to go for it, even if they too are married. Find greater intimacy with someone else? The world encourages us to find fulfillment regardless of the cost and consequences. Irreconcilable differences plague every couple brought together in the bond of marriage, because every couple is also bonded by sin. There is no way around the work involved to make marriage work. Great marriages don't happen by chance, but by intentionality and hard work.

If marriage is both an incredible blessing and a constant burden, how can we make it work? The answer, once again, is found in declaring over marriage, "it's not about me." Let's talk about three areas where this statement is critical.

1) It's critical to say about your role in marriage, "it's not about me."

If you want a manual for how marriage works, I know of none better than Ephesians 5:21-33.

This section of Scripture starts with everyone's favorite action verb - "submit."

"**Submit** to one another out of reverence for Christ" (Ephesians 5:21).

Who is called to submit? The wife or the husband? Both! Both husband and wife are called to submit, and they do so recognizing what Christ first did for them. Every time a spouse submits, they have the opportunity to stand in awe of the sacrificial love of Christ. Jesus came and submitted to the Father's will, submitted to what was necessary to save the world. In doing so, He submitted to death on the cross. Jesus did this out of love for you.

Out of love and reverence for Jesus, spouses have the opportunity each day to submit to one another. In doing this, they are the visual Gospel of what it is to be loved by Jesus Himself.

But submission looks different for the husband than it does for the wife, based on the God-given roles of marriage.

The husband has been assigned the immense task of being like Jesus, and leading his spouse and whole family. Christian leadership in this role is not about barking orders for supper, a TV remote, and a preferred activity for the weekend. Leadership in Christ's world means that the higher you are, the lower you are willing to go. The King of kings allowed Himself to be considered a criminal so He could die our death. If you are a husband, you are assigned to what seems like an impossible task - be like Jesus. Be willing to die if that's what your spouse needs.

Paul put it this way: "Husbands, love your wives, just as Christ loved the church and gave himself up for her" (Ephesians 5:25).

Congratulations husband, your mantle is leader. But to clarify, it means you are lead servant. Your decisions, your activities, your words, and your prayers are all intended to serve your spouse and prop her up. You have an incredible responsibility that will require the strength of God.

Consider for a moment if husband hears, "I am the leader" without also recognizing that when it comes to the role, "it's not about me"?

I've had the privilege to do marriage counseling. It's an honor to point people to God's paradigm for marriage, so they can see the beauty and blessing intended. I'll never forget one counseling session. A husband and wife had a disagreement, and the husband turned to me and said, "Tell her she has to do what I say, because I am the leader." From that moment I realized I had some teaching to do on what kind of leader God intended.

When leadership goes wrong, men look like Homer Simpson. Homer used his financial position on Marge's birthday to buy Marge a bowling ball. Why? It wasn't because Marge loved bowling. She expressively told Homer, "I've never bowled in my life!" It's because Homer loved bowling and wanted a new ball. It's why the bowling ball even had Homer's name engraved on it.[1]

In contrast, being a lead servant means sticking up for your way when your bride's wellbeing is at stake. Being a lead servant means if anyone is doing the hardest work and sacrificing the most, it should be you. Being a lead servant means evaluating job opportunities, purchases, time spent on hobbies through a filter that asks, "How will this benefit my bride?" This is a glimpse of what it means to be a Christian husband fulfilling your leadership role.

Scripture shows us two epic failures when it comes to husbands as lead servants.

The first happens in the Garden of Eden. You probably know the story. Eve is tempted by the snake and eats the forbidden fruit. But where is Adam? Scripture says, "She took some and ate it. She also gave some to her husband, **who was with her,** and he ate it" (Genesis 3:6). Adam was right there next to Eve the whole time! As Eve is dialoguing, he has the responsibility as lead servant to speak up. He should have said, "Hey babe, we know God. He's only been good, and hasn't lied to us yet. We do not know this snake! Let's skedaddle!" But Adam was passive, and failed at his role of lead servant.

Passivity is the sin of the lead servant. Every Christian husband should fight against it.

The second account is with Abraham. God promised a child, and years into that promise his wife, Sarah, was not pregnant. So Sarah had an idea, and she suggested, "The Lord has kept me from having children. Go, sleep with my slave; perhaps I can build a family through her" (Genesis 16:2). What was Abraham supposed to do as lead servant? He should have said, "Never! God never requires us to sin for His will to be accomplished. We need to have patience." But Abraham didn't stand against his wife's suggestion, and failed at his role of lead servant.

The consequences of these two accounts cannot be understated. The human race fell from grace when Adam failed to lead. A whole nation was born as enemies to God's people because Abraham failed to lead.

There is only one Hero who demonstrates beautifully what lead servant looks like. It's Jesus who is the role model for every husband. He disputes with Peter about the inevitability of the cross. He spoke up and said, in opposition to Peter, "Get behind me, Satan! You are a stumbling block to me; you do not have in mind the concerns of God, but merely human concerns" (Matthew 16:23). Jesus proved that leadership is lonely. In His hour of need, He had no one else to support Him, no one else who was there. Jesus proved that the leadership mantle comes with great sacrifice. In order to put our needs first, Jesus would bear the ridicule, the flogging, the crown of thorns, and the cross. No one understood His servant leadership in the moment. No one caught Him in the midst of His suffering. But on the other side of the empty tomb, we stand amazed by the nobility of what He did. He saved us, and He is the atoning sacrifice for the sins of the world.

Husband, be like Jesus. Show her a leader worth following, who regularly models sacrifice. Be willing to die that she might live.

The wife's assigned role is to be like the church, which follows the lead of Jesus. Paul put it this way, "Now as the church submits to Christ, so also wives should submit to their husbands in everything" (Ephesians 5:24).

Perhaps it's easiest to start out explaining what this does NOT mean. It does not mean a wife cannot give her counsel and aid to situations. It does not mean she has to agree with her husband on every matter. It certainly does not mean she is inferior to her husband. Scripture is clear that men and women are co-equals and co-heirs.[2]

To get into what this might look like, let's talk about baseball. In the game of baseball there is an order that exists between pitcher and catcher. The catcher gives the pitcher signs for which ball to throw - whether it be a fastball, change-up, curveball, cutter, or knuckleball. The pitcher follows this orderly arrangement, and agrees to throw whatever the catcher gives the sign for. Yet, there are times when the pitcher shakes his head, and asks for another sign. If they can't agree on strategy, sometimes there is a meeting on the mound. But for the sake of order, the catcher tells the pitcher what to throw. In this arrangement there is no question about who is the better player. For that matter, there is no question about who is smarter, stronger, or anything else. This is simply the order of baseball.

God, who is a God of order, established an orderly system for the household. Wife, your role is to follow the lead of your husband. You are intended to be a servant follower. Sometimes you may need to shake off the call. Sometimes there may need to be a meeting at the mound. But in general, let your husband lead.

Just as there are horrible consequences when husbands do not fulfill their role, so there are horrible consequences when wives do not fulfill their role.

We considered Adam and Abraham failing to fulfill their role. So let's also consider the God-given role of Eve and Sarah, and how it went awry. Both of them were leading, but in the wrong direction. Let's look at the passages again. **"She took some and ate it. She also gave some to her husband**, who was with her, and he ate it" (Genesis 3:6). Based on her role as servant follower she had the responsibility to consult with her husband before this action and to respect his counsel. The same goes with Sarah who led by saying, **"Go, sleep with my slave**; perhaps I can build a family through her" (Genesis 16:2). Before coming to this conclusion, she had the responsibility to consult with her husband and to respect his counsel. Instead, both tried to coerce their husbands into sin. They both failed to fulfill their role as a servant follower.

Modern culture struggles mightily with male leadership. Partly, because of a history of abuse of power. Partly, because of our sinful nature, we do not want to submit or follow anyone - husbands and God included. Culture rarely presents a winsome male leader, preferring caricatures like Homer Simpson, Peter Griffin, and Michael Scott. And the consequences of a lack of male leadership are staggering. One out of four children grow up in a home without a father.[3] The spiritual life of the next generation limps along, and may be lost without a father leading his family toward Jesus.[4] Society is plagued with problems that stem from a void of male leadership, which include sexual temptation, identity issues, and poverty.[5]

When a wife's role goes wrong, it leads to condescension, mocking, and guilt-tripping. Condescension breaks the clear command of God for respect to husbands. Mocking does the same. Guilt-tripping creates an avenue for a husband to act as pathetic as his spouse intimates he is.

So what would it look like to fulfill the servant follower role in a God-pleasing way?

The early Christian Church was fueled by the Holy Spirit and on fire for the Lord. They listened to Christ's command to preach and teach the good news to all people. Peter and the Apostles would not keep quiet about the resurrection of Jesus. Yet, they were threatened, imprisoned, and punished for following Jesus. Peter, after being imprisoned for preaching, was threatened to no longer do what Christ said and stop preaching. He resisted and said, "We must obey God rather than human beings" (Acts 2:29). Others, who were persecuted and flogged, rejoiced for being considered worthy to suffer for the name of Jesus.[6] They were willing to sacrifice because Jesus had sacrificed for them. They were willing to follow Jesus and submit to His will all the way to their own deaths, as eleven of the twelve Apostles died a martyr's death.[7]

Wife, be like the church. Follow your husband's lead, and show him respect and support as he carries the leadership mantle. Be willing to die if that's what following this godly lead requires.

2) It's critical when it comes to conflict resolution to remember "it's not about me."

Conflict will happen in every marriage because men and women were made differently.[8] Conflict can arise because of a disagreement. Conflict also happens because of sins against each other.

Traveling to different countries is eye-opening. I had a chance to go the Czech Republic while my sister was doing mission work there. I learned that when you get sick in the Czech Republic, one of the remedies is to go to a spa town and drink mineral water. Top that off with an herbal alcohol called Becherovka, and you may be cured of that cold in no time! I considered how different that was than in the States. Here the remedies are antibiotics, chicken noodle soup, crackers, and binging some TV. Which solution to sickness was better? I don't know, but I knew which one I would prefer.

Learning from different cultures helps us to understand sometimes things are not better or worse - they are simply different.

The spice of marriage is working out your differences, and coming to solutions rather than stalemates. This can be a challenge, to say the least!

When a conflict does arise it's incredibly important to remember "it's not about me."

Scripture advises us in our relationships with others, and especially our spouse, "Make every effort to keep the unity of the Spirit through the bond of peace" (Ephesians 4:3). But how do we do that when we see things so differently, or have been sinned against by our spouse?

The saddest thing I ever see as pastor is impenitence. Impenitence is when a person says to God and to others, "I'm not changing. I don't care what my spouse says, my pastor says, or even what God says. The problem is with them. Until they change, or until the circumstances or the explanation of my behavior changes - we cannot go forward." I believe impenitence is the root cause for the majority of divorces. An impenitent spouse is saying, "I won't listen to God or to you. I don't care." The fruit of that impenitence may be adultery, may be an addiction, or it may be abuse of some sort. Yet, at one point or another they determined, "I'm doing it my way, and no one is going to change me."

One of the greatest things to celebrate is repentance. Even angels in heaven throw a party over that.[9] Repentance is admitting you've done something wrong, and you have something to work on. Repentance is going to God to seek His mercy and forgiveness, but then also to listen to His guidance going forward. Repentance is at the core of two sinners who learn to live with each other and love each other. Repentance is essential on both sides of any conflict.

Repentance is seen clearly in the woman caught in adultery. She was found guilty of sin, and she didn't claim innocence. She found mercy and forgiveness in Jesus, who said He does not condemn her. She then was encouraged to a new path as she was told to leave her life of sin.[10]

A repentant heart is willing to start with what could have been done better in any conflict. Even if the conflict arose because ninety-five percent of the problem was on someone else. They hurt you. They said or did something to make you mad. Repentance is about owning the five percent of the problem that is yours. It's starting with yourself, with the acknowledgement that most of the time it takes two to tango.

But acknowledging we have something to own in a conflict is a bitter pill to swallow for an arrogant, sinful heart. So how do we get there?

One of the most powerful stories Jesus told was that of a servant who owed an unpayable debt.[11] In Jesus' day you couldn't just declare bankruptcy and start over with a knock to your credit score. No, in Jesus' day you could be thrown in prison, and your spouse and children could be sold into slavery until that debt was paid. The servant had an idea that was the long shot of long shots. He would go to his master, begging on his knees, and simply ask him to cancel the debt. The day came, he got on his knees and begged and…the master agreed! There is winning the lottery, and then there is this! This has to be the happiest day of the man's life. He can go home and proudly announce, "Hey babe, guess what!? I'm not going to prison! You and the kids don't have to worry about slavery! And any money I make from here on out is ours to keep! The debt has been canceled! Yahoo!!"

You know who Jesus told that story about? You and me. We go to God with an unpayable debt of sin. There is no way we can make up for a single sin, much less the sins of our lifetime. Yet, our gracious God cancels all our debts because of the cross of Jesus Christ. No immediate penalty. No impending doom or worries of hell. No guilt hanging over our heads. We have complete freedom that should make us dance and sing and be overjoyed! Freedom, peace, love, and joy are ours because of the grace of our God!

And what we have received from God we give to others. It has been said that "hurt people hurt people." But it is also true that "forgiven people forgive people."

Jesus' story, unfortunately, didn't have such a heartwarming ending. The servant did not want to give what he had received. So his master put the debt back on him. He immediately threw him into jail where he would be tortured. And Jesus conclusion to the story? "This is how my heavenly Father will treat each of you unless you forgive your brother or sister from your heart" (Matthew 18:35).

If the love of God doesn't compel us to get this right, surely the punishments of God should make us rethink any act of unforgiveness.

What does it mean to forgive?

The answer to this could be a book itself. So here are the cliff notes.

First let's start with what forgiveness is NOT. Forgiveness is NOT…waiting for an apology, waiting until you feel like forgiving, forgetting what was done or condoning it, or holding their wrong against them in order to get your way the next time. And forgiveness is NOT easy. Forgiveness also is NOT enabling. You can forgive someone without things being the same. If someone steal from work, can they be forgiven? Of course! The blood of Jesus pays for theft. Do they still have a job? Probably not. In marriage boundaries can be put up after a sin has occurred, and it doesn't mean a spouse hasn't forgiven the sin. It simply means a spouse is not ok enabling bad behavior.

And now what IS forgiveness? Forgiveness IS…paying the debt that occurred. Do you remember the King James Version of the Lord's Prayer which said, "Forgive us our debts as we forgive our debtors"?[12] That's what you do in forgiveness, you pay the debt the other cannot. Forgiveness IS…a process. Because you will not be able to forget what was done to you, as often as that hurt comes up, you will have to forgive it again. You don't have to tell the person again, but think of it like mental wack-a-mole. The hurt pops up, you whack it with forgiveness - pops up again, forgive it again. Forgive it again and again and again until hopefully that thought is not so frequent, and its grip loosens around your mind and your emotions. Forgiveness IS…a decision and action. It is not a feeling. Forgiveness reminds me of this quote by C.S. Lewis where he says about love, "Do not waste time bothering whether you 'love' your neighbor; act as if you did. When you are behaving as if you loved someone, you will presently come to love him."[13] So I too would say don't waste time on wondering how you feel about forgiving others. Forgive them, and let your emotions catch up with your action. Forgiveness IS…a beautiful journey to the cross. First you go there to see all your sins paid for in full! But from there you leave ready to give to others what you have received. Because forgiveness IS…possible through Christ.

You and I will be asked to forgive some pretty big hurts in our lifetime. This is not easy, and many of the deepest hurts may come from our spouse. Yet, it is an opportunity to find joy in the forgiveness Christ won for us, and to do for others what He did for us. Yes, "forgiven people forgive people."

One great suggestion to handling conflict in a marriage is having a conflict resolution plan. A conflict resolution plan may look like this:

1) The offended party will look for the right time and the right way to address the offense.
2) The offended party brings up the issue by beginning the discussion with prayer.
3) The offended party focuses on the issue, and does not attack the person. "Always" and "never" will be avoided when talking about the other's actions, as they rule out any progress that has been made.
4) Both parties will practice active listening, where the other spouse repeats back what they heard. Think of active listening through the lens of a drive-through order. The one receiving the order repeats back the order, until the customer is assured it is correct. Though repeating back what you heard might seem tedious, it can really help fight against misunderstanding each other.
5) The first one to say "I'm sorry" wins. Often it leads to the other person apologizing for their part, as again, it takes two to tango.

6) Next steps to avoid this conflict in the future are discussed and agreed upon.

7) The other spouse closes with prayer.

If we truly live with a "it's not about me" mentality in marriage, it won't really matter who is right or who is wrong. What will matter is that reconciliation happens, and that a plan to show love to one another is established.

3) It's critical when it comes to love languages to remember "it's not about me."

The love you want is often the love you give. If you merely follow the golden rule, "love your neighbor as yourself," you will fail at loving your spouse properly.

It was the first day of our married lives together. We honeymooned in Las Vegas, and I was ready to explore the city with my beautiful bride. I was up at 6am, but I wanted to let my wife sleep in so I waited until 8am. As soon as my decided time arrived, I flung wide our bedroom doors, blared loud music, and proudly announced our adventure was about to begin. To understate my wife's reaction, she did not have the same idea in mind. She clarified that to her, our honeymoon was about resting, not about going on adventures. This was one of many times where I recognized I was made differently from my spouse.

What I wanted wasn't what she wanted. What she wanted isn't what I wanted. So where would we go or not go from here?

Over the years we've learned a lot about what each other likes and dislikes. "The 5 Love Languages" by Gary Chapman has been incredibly helpful in learning about each other. If you are not familiar with the five, they are 1) Acts of Service, 2) Words of Affirmation, 3) Quality Time, 4) Physical Touch, and 5) Receiving Gifts.[14]

My wife's top two are Words of Affirmation and Receiving Gifts. These are my bottom two, and they don't come naturally for me.

If I were to make excuses, I would talk about my childhood. In my family of origin, Acts of Service reigned supreme for how to love one another. On my mom's birthday, when she can ask for whatever she wants, she often asks my dad for things like cleaning the garage or painting the laundry room. So in our household, we tried to work hard for each other as a way of showing love. What we didn't work so hard at were Words of Affirmation.

When I got married, I was ready to put in the work of love. I selfishly thought I could outwork anyone. Surely, my spouse would recognize the benefit of all the Acts of Service I was prepared to do. Need the garage cleaned? On it! Need the grass mowed? No problem! How about meals made for the week and put into Tupperware? I'm your man.

But do you want kind-toned, filtered words like honey and sweetie while I'm in work mode? I stink at this. Over eighteen years of marriage, and I'm still a work in progress. My wife's love language preference is so strong when it comes to words that if I built a mansion for her with my bare hands, but didn't use nice words doing it - she wouldn't want it.

So I have work to do. I'm currently working on tone, word choice, note-writing and small gift giving. I still screw up. But I hope my wife would say I've made progress not only in my understanding of what she needs, but also in my frequency of getting it right.

Where do you need to put in the work? Are you giving the love you want, without recognizing that your spouse's love language might not be the same as yours?

When we look at love languages and say, "it's not about me," those differences are not annoyances but opportunities. An understanding of your spouse's primary love language gives you a blueprint to get love right. It's an opportunity for your spouse to truly know how much you love them as you put in the work of love.

God does this well. The grace He gives you often looks different from the grace He gives your siblings, your parents, and your co-workers. That's because He knows exactly who you are, and exactly what you would like. I imagine my corner of heaven and my job in heaven will look different than yours. Because the God who made us uniquely will continue to treat us this way. He loves us with a unique love based on who we are and what we need.

When it comes to marriage, it's been a privilege of mine to conduct weddings. A famous section of Scripture that I get to preach on is 1 Corinthians 13. It's the *love* chapter. It gives beautiful descriptions of love such as…patient, kind, not self-seeking, keeping no record of wrongs and so on. But one of the concluding thoughts is this, "Now I know **in part**; then I shall know fully, even as I am fully known" (1 Corinthians 13:12). When I preach on this, I dig in on the thought that we know "in part."

Wedding celebrations correlate to Biblical pictures of heaven.[15] But eating and drinking with family and friends here on earth is only a glimpse, only knowing "in part" what heaven will be like. Heaven is the wedding feast that never ends. Isaiah the prophet tells us heaven is filled with the best of meats and finest of wines.[16] John in his book Revelation describes wonders beyond our imagination.[17] The best party on earth is merely knowing "in part" the glories that are in store.

So also we only know God's love "in part." He knows us fully and loves us completely, but we cannot claim the same. Because we know "in part" we often attach our primary love to less-than things like spouses, kids, possessions, and even pets. These gifts were meant to point us to His love, not take the place of it. His love is the meal that satisfies, everything else and everyone else is merely supplemental.

But a spouse might be greater than an orange. A good spouse I might upgrade to a Chipotle burrito. And they, more than anyone else on the planet, have the opportunities to show us glimpses of God's love.

If you are married, may it start with you. May you love your spouse so well that they get a glimpse of God. May they even think on certain days, "this must be what it's like to be loved by God." But even on those days may you know this is just a glimpse of God's love – this is only knowing "in part." May you be empowered by the Spirit and fueled by the thought that when it comes to marriage, "it's not about me."

Like everything else we've considered, marriage is simply another opportunity to glorify God and love your neighbor.

Soli Deo Gloria

STUDY QUESTIONS

1) When you first got married were there any unrealistic expectations about what your spouse should do? Has anyone ever had unrealistic expectations about what you could do?

2) What are the most incredible blessings about marriage for you? What are the most difficult parts of marriage for you?

3) Read Ephesians 5:21-33. How do you feel about God's design for Christian marriage? How do you feel about your role inside of marriage? Where could you currently work to improve based on your role in marriage?

4) Think of a time where you found someone unwilling to change. What does repentance look like for you? Is there anything your spouse has been asking you to work on? What is that?

5) Do you currently have a conflict resolution plan? What do you think of the plan suggested in this chapter? What might you change about the plan?

6) Of the 5 love languages, do you know your preferred love language? Do you know the top love language for your spouse?

What are some things you might do for your spouse based on their love language?

7) What stands out to you as the most important way God showed or shows us love? In what ways do you hope your spouse is seeing God's love through you?

CONCLUSION

The big questions of "how" and "why" probably remain. Why should I live the rest of my life saying, "it's not about me"? How can I have the strength to apply this to principle?

My advice here: wrap yourself up in the love of Jesus. Read your Bible daily. Worship weekly. Pray regularly. Get to know who He is more and more, and He'll continue to wow you and give you strength.

See the reality in Jesus is this: He made his whole life about loving and redeeming you. I consider what John said about this work: "Greater love has no one than this: to lay down one's life for one's friend" (John 13:1). To riff on this idea, what I believe is this: there is no greater love than that of one who says "it's not about me" because they made it about you. And this is what Jesus did. His life was ALL about you. His cross was ALL about you. His resurrection was ALL about you. His activity right now is ALL about you. His love is ALL about you.

And because of that love you don't have to spend the rest of your life wondering if you matter. You matter to God. Jesus made his whole life revolve around you, to ransom you.

So what if we in return said, "God I love you too." What if we in return emptied ourselves, and made the rest of our lives about loving Him. I believe we would give God great glory, and greatly help our neighbor. May God strengthen you to live a life that says, "it's not about me." Let it say to our God, "it's ALL about You!"

A closing prayer: *"Dear Jesus, how great is Your love. While I'm still searching out the lengths of it, I've seen again how you emptied Yourself that I might be blessed and saved. Thank you Jesus. I confess it's so hard to turn the attention away from myself. But by the power of the Holy Spirit I ask that I might. That like You, I might be willing to empty myself to glorify Your name, and help my neighbor. Forgive me for the times a radical pursuit of myself has hurt others and dishonored You. Help me to find peace, joy, and a new direction as I've heard Your Word. Now let it take root in my life. Amen."*

NOTES

Chapter 1: The Problem

1. American Cancer Society. American Heart Association. American Lung Association.
2. Merriam-Webster, September 7, 2023, https://www.merriam-webster.com/dictionary/narcissist.
3. Charles Freeman (2014). *Egypt, Greece, and Rome: civilizations of the ancient Mediterranean* (Third ed.). Oxford. ISBN 978-0199651917. OCLC 868077503.
4. Suetonius, "Nero" 31; *Pliny's Natural History* XXXIV.45.
5. Jackson Spielvogel and David Redles, "Hitler's Racial Ideology: Content and Occult Sources," https://www.museumoftolerance.com/education/archives-and-reference-library/online-resources/simon-wiesenthal-center-annual-volume-3/annual-3-chapter-9.html.
6. Peter Preskar, "The Prolific Love Life of Genghis Khan," November 3, 2020, https://short-history.com/love-life-of-genghis-khan-9d000b47c774.
7. Steve Denning, "Lest We Forget: Why We Had A Financial Crisis," November 22, 2011, https://www.forbes.com/sites/stevedenning/2011/11/22/5086/?sh=3e17de3bf92f.
8. Matthew 18:1-4, Mark 9:33-36, Luke 9:46-47, Luke 22:24, NIV 2011.
9. Matthew 7:7, NIV 2011.
10. Mark 11:24, NIV 2011.
11. James 4:15, NIV 2011.

12. Matthew 19:20, NIV 2011.

13. Daniel Schorn, "Transcript: Tom Brady, Part 3," November 4, 2005, https://www.cbsnews.com/news/transcript-tom-brady-part-3/.

14. Jay Stone, *The Ottawa Citizen*, December 2005. https://quoteinvestigator.com/2022/11/09/rich-famous/.

Chapter 2: The Solution

1. Genesis 3:15, NIV 2011.

2. Hebrews 4:15, NIV 2011.

3. 1 John 2:2, NIV 2011.

4. Romans 3:23-25, NIV 2011.

5. Romans 5:8, NIV 2011.

6. Hebrews 13:5, NIV 2011.

7. Romans 8:28, NIV 2011.

8. Psalm 23:1, NIV 2011.

9. Revelation 21:4, NIV 2011.

10. 1 Corinthians 13:12, NIV 2011.

11. Psalm 73:25-26, NIV 2011.

12. Ephesians 2:8-9, NIV 2011.

13. Romans 12:1, NIV 2011.

14. Ephesians 2:1-5, NIV 2011.

15. 1 Corinthians 10:31, NIV 2011.

Chapter 3: Power

1. Bernie Pitzel, "Be Like Mike," music by Ira Antelis and Steve Shafer, broadcast date August 8th, 1991, campaign created by Bayer Bess Vanderwarker.

2. OfficialHoophall, "Michael Jordan's Basketball Hall of Fame Enshrinement Speech," February 21, 2012, https://www.youtube.com/watch?v=XLzBMGXfK4c.

3. 1 Samuel 17:4-7, NIV 2011.

4. "Battle of Thermopylae," September 23, 2023, https://en.wikipedia.org/wiki/Battle_of_Thermopylae#cite_note-15.

5. Judges 8:22-27, NIV 2011.

6. Nina Totenberg and Sarah McCammon, "Supreme Court overturns Roe v. Wade, ending right to abortion upheld for decades," June 24, 2022, https://www.npr.org/2022/06/24/1102305878/supreme-court-abortion-roe-v-wade-decision-overturn.

7. Martin Luther, *Luther's Catechism*, (Northwestern Publishing House, 1982), 4.

8. It's hard to beat the practicality and reliability of a Prius. Fifty miles per gallon and known for lasting three hundred thousand miles - incredible! No, I was never a Toyota salesman.

9. This common Christian lie comes from a misinterpretation of 1 Corinthians 10:13, NIV 2011. In this passage Paul is stating when tempted we can have strength to find a way out of that temptation.

10. Job 38-41, NIV 2011.

11. Isaiah 59:1, NIV 2011.

12. "The Twelve Steps," https://www.aa.org/the-twelve-steps.

13. Romans 7:14-25, NIV 2011.

14. Hebrews 4:14, NIV 2011.

15. John 19:30, NIV 2011.

16. 1 Corinthians 15:4, NIV 2011.

17. Romans 1:16, NIV 2011.

18. Jenni Carlson, "Oklahoma City Thunder: Transcript of Monty Williams' moving speech," February 19, 2016, https://www.oklahoman.com/story/sports/columns/jenni-carlson/2016/02/19/oklahoma-city-thunder-transcript-of-monty-williams-moving-speech/60691505007/.

Chapter 4: Sex

1. Bill Cosby. "Chocolate Cake For Breakfast." *Himself*. Motown Records. 2006. CD.

2. Bill Cosby. *Fatherhood*, (Berkley Publishing Group, 1987).

3. Eric Levenson and Aaron Cooper, "Bill Cosby guilty on all three counts in indecent assault trial," April 26, 2018,

https://www.cnn.com/2018/04/26/us/bill-cosby-trial/index.html#:~:text=A jury found Bill Cosby,a Philadelphia suburb in 2004.

4. Ray Sanchez, Sonia Moghe, and Kristina Sguegli, "Bill Cosby is a free man after Pennsylvania Supreme Court overturns sex assault conviction," June 30, 2021, https://www.cnn.com/2021/06/30/us/bill-cosby-to-be-released/index.html.

5. Jenna Schoenefeld. "Bill Cosby Trial: Court Sides With Judy Huth, Who Accused Bill Cosby of a 1975 Sexual Assault," June 21, 2022, https://www.nytimes.com/live/2022/06/21/arts/bill-cosby-verdict-judy-huth.

6. Lee Strobel. June 11, 2013, https://twitter.com/LeeStrobel/status/355433881001934849#

7. The Associated Press, "Law firm details sexual misconduct by global ministry leader Ravi Zacharias," February 12, 2021, https://www.nbcnews.com/news/us-news/law-firm-details-sexual-misconduct-global-ministry-leader-ravi-zacharias-n1257629#.

8. Judges 14-16, NIV 2011.

9. Judges 13:4-7, NIV 2011.

10. Judges 16:1, NIV 2011.

11. *Christian Worship: A Lutheran Hymnal*, (Northwestern Publishing House, 1993), 142.

12. Centers for Disease Control and Prevention, "Fast Facts: Preventing Sexual Violence," June, 22, 2022, https://www.cdc.gov/violenceprevention/sexualviolence/fastfact.html.

13. 1 Samuel 13:14, NIV 2011.

14. Psalm 73:26, NIV 2011.

15. Genesis 16:13, NIV 2011.

16. Romans 8:11, NIV 2011.

17. Collins Dictionary, https://www.collinsdictionary.com/us/dictionary/english/corinthianize#.

18. John 19:26, John 11:5, John 11, NIV 2011.

19. Matthew 18:18, NIV 2011.

20. Galatians 6:1-2, NIV 2011.

21. Romans 1:24-27, NIV 2011.

22. Psalm 51:5, NIV 2011.

23. 1 John 2:2, NIV 2011.

24. John 8:11, Hebrews 10:26-27, NIV 2011.

25. Romans 7:14-25, NIV 2011.

26. Hebrews 4:15, NIV 2011.

27. John 1:14, NIV 2011.

Chapter 5: Money

1. Chris Columbus. 1992. *Home Alone 2: Lost In New York*. 20th Century Fox.

2. Prakash Joshi Pax. "Why Alexander The Great Made These 3 Strange Wishes In His Deathbed," January 17, 2021, https://medium.com/lessons-from-history/why-alexander-the-great-made-these-3-strange-wishes-in-his-deathbed-ed7712af985d.

3. Lizzie Smiley. "Five Keys to Discovering Your God-Given Purpose," January 30, 2017, https://www.createapeacefulhome.com/five-keys-to-discovering-your-god-given-purpose-in-this-world/

4. Dave Ramsey. *The Total Money Makeover: Classic Edition: A Proven Plan for Financial Fitness*, (Thomas Nelson, 2003).

5. Luke 12:13-21, NIV 2011.

6. Special Collections & Archives Research Center. "The Gutenberg Press," http://scarc.library.oregonstate.edu/omeka/exhibits/show/mcdonald/incunabula/gutenberg/#:~:text=By 1440 Gutenberg had established,of indulgences for the Church.

7. Statista Research Department. "Countries with the highest average wealth per adult worldwide in 2022," September 28, 2023, https://www.statista.com/statistics/203941/countries-with-the-highest-wealth-per-adult/#:~:text=In 2022, Switzerland led the,per adult, followed by Australia.

8. Pew Research Center. "In U.S., Decline of Christianity Continues at Rapid Pace," October 17, 2019, https://www.pewresearch.org/religion/2019/10/17/in-u-s-decline-of-christianity-continues-at-rapid-pace/.

9. Mike Homes. "What Would Happen if the Church Tithed?" June 15, 2021, https://relevantmagazine.com/faith/church/what-would-happen-if-church-tithed/.

10. https://www.academiacristo.com/.

Chapter 6: Pain

1. Adrian Warnock. "God Breaks Those He Wants To Make Great," October 18, 2009, https://www.patheos.com/blogs/adrianwarnock/2009/10/god-breaks-those-he-wants-to-make-great/.

2. Centers for Disease Control and Prevention. "Understanding the Opioid Overdose Epidemic," August 8, 2023, https://www.cdc.gov/opioids/basics/epidemic.html.

3. Romans 8:20, NIV 2011.

4. Job 38-40, NIV 2011.

5. Ephesians 1:4-10, NIV 2011.

6. Corrie ten Boom. "Life is but a Weaving," February 21, 2018, https://thepoetryplace.wordpress.com/2018/02/21/life-is-but-a-weaving-the-tapestry-poem-by-corrie-ten-boom/.

7. 1 Corinthians 13:12, NIV 2011.

8. Francis Pieper. *Christian Dogmatics: Volume 1*, (Concordia Publishing House, 1950) 533-537.

9. Jerry Bridges. *Trusting God: Even When Life Hurts*, (Navpress, 1989).

10. Isaiah 53:3, NIV 2011.

11. 2 Corinthians 4:7, NIV 2011.

Chapter 7: Church

1. Matthew 4:19, NIV 2011.

2. Eric Thomas. Eric Thomas Quote: "To get to that next level, you gotta learn to get comfortable being uncomfortable." (quotefancy.com).

3. ChurchTrainerGroup. "The Power of an Invite," https://churchtrainer.com/the-power-of-an-invite/#:~:text=What initially brought you to church?&text=3-4% Had a need met by the church.&text=70-85% Invited by a relative or friend!

4. Acts 9:19-31, NIV 2011.

5. Acts 19:16-24, NIV 2011.

6. 2 Corinthians 11, NIV 2011.

7. R.C. Sproul. *What Is Repentance?* (Ligonier Ministries, 2019).

8. Acts 2:42-47, NIV 2011.

9. Matthew 26:26-29, NIV 2011.

10. Titus 3:5, NIV 2011.

11. Romans 10:17, NIV 2011.

12. 2 Corinthians 5:20, Colossians 4:4, Acts 19:8, NIV 2011.

13. 1 Corinthians 1:27, NIV 2011.

14. 1 Corinthians 3:7, NIV 2011.

15. James 3:1, NIV 2011.

16. Hebrews 13:17, NIV 2011.

17. Romans 16:17, NIV 2011.

18. 1 Corinthians 12:21, NIV 2011.

19. Jeffrey Jones. "U.S. Charitable Donations Rebound; Volunteering Still Down," January 11, 2022, https://news.gallup.com/poll/388574/charitable-donations-rebound-volunteering-down.aspx#:~:text=Thirty-five percent of Americans,readings in 2008 and 2009.

20. Dwight L. Moody. https://www.azquotes.com/quote/694531.

21. Romans 11:33, Isaiah 55:9, NIV 2011.

Chapter 8: Identity

1. Sarah Keller. "Identity Fraud Losses Totaled $43 Billion in 2022, Affecting 40 Million U.S. Adults," March 28, 2023, https://javelinstrategy.com/press-release/identity-fraud-losses-totaled-43-billion-2022-affecting-40-million-us-adults.

2. Romans 5:2, NIV 2011.

3. Clay Edgar. "If Earth Was a Grain of Sand," June 19, 2018, https://medium.com/@clay.c.edgar/if-earth-was-a-grain-of-sand-22ea58f43d5e.

4. C.S. Lewis. *Mere Christianity*, (HarperSanFransico, 1980).

5. Barna Group. "Sharing Faith Is Increasingly Optional to Christians," May 15, 2018, https://www.barna.com/research/sharing-faith-increasingly-optional-christians/.

6. Aaron Earls. "Christians Don't Share Faith With Unchurched Friends," September 9, 2021, https://research.lifeway.com/2021/09/09/christians-dont-share-faith-with-unchurched-friends/.

7. Theodore Roosevelt. https://www.goodreads.com/quotes/34690-people-don-t-care-how-much-you-know-until-they-know

8. Dailymail.comReporter. "Woman has spent more than $50,000 on plastic surgery to look like her idol Jessica Rabbit - getting multiple lip injections and fake SIZE H boobs - and she's planning to get even more done," April 16, 2018, https://www.dailymail.co.uk/femail/article-5621189/Woman-spends-50K-plastic-surgery-look-like-Jessica-Rabbit.html

9. Andie Reeves. "Watch this Ford Mustang transform into a boat," September 21, 2023, https://supercarblondie.com/ford-mustang-boat-on-water/.

Chapter 9: Control

1. WebMD Editorial Contributors. "Signs of Controlling Behavior," September 7, 2022, https://www.webmd.com/mental-health/signs-controlling-behavior.

2. Emma Dibdin. "Need to Control Everything? This May Be Why," March 29, 2022, https://psychcentral.com/blog/why-you-need-to-control-everything#why-you-need-to-control.

3. Amanda Hetler. "The Great Resignation: Everything you need to know," July 3, 2023, https://www.techtarget.com/whatis/feature/The-Great-Resignation-Everything-you-need-to-know.

4. Jeffrey Jones. "U.S. Church Attendance Still Lower Than Pre-Pandemic," June 26, 2023, https://news.gallup.com/poll/507692/church-attendance-lower-pre-pandemic.aspx.

5. Alison Brunier. "COVID-19 pandemic triggers 25% increase in prevalence of anxiety and depression worldwide," March 2, 2022, https://www.who.int/news/item/02-03-2022-covid-19-pandemic-triggers-25-increase-in-prevalence-of-anxiety-and-depression-worldwide.

6. Wikipedia. "1992 United States men's Olympic basketball team," https://en.wikipedia.org/wiki/1992_United_States_men's_Olympic_basketball_team.

7. C.S. Lewis. *The Joyful Christian*, (Scribner, 1996).

8. Wikipedia. "Copernican heliocentrism," https://en.wikipedia.org/wiki/Copernican_heliocentrism#:~:text=Copernicus held that the Earth,the universe, but near it.

9. Wikipedia. "Phases of Venus,"
    https://en.wikipedia.org/wiki/Phases_of_Venus.
10. Wikipedia. "Hubble Space Telescope,"
    https://en.wikipedia.org/wiki/Hubble_Space_Telescope#Black_holes.
11. Isaiah 55:3, NIV 2011.
12. Abbie Strong. *Facebook*, October 12, 2022,
    https://www.facebook.com/GraceLutheranDowntown/photos/a.1015019466
    5119440/10159682624349440/.
13. Genesis 15:13, NIV 2011.
14. Daniel 4:33, NIV 2011.
15. Acts 12:21-23, NIV 2011.
16. Saint Augustine.
    https://www.brainyquote.com/quotes/saint_augustine_165165.

Chapter 10: Children

1. Psalm 127:3, NIV 2011.
2. Psalm 139:16, NIV 2011.
3. Timothy Keller. *Counterfeit Gods*, (Dutton, 2009) xviii.
4. Genesis 37:4, 2 Samuel 13:15, 2 Samuel 13:22, NIV 2011.
5. Job 2:10, NIV 2011.
6. Wikipedia. "Richard Williams (tennis coach),"
    https://en.wikipedia.org/wiki/Richard_Williams_(tennis_coach).
7. Genesis 39:2, 9, NIV 2011.
8. Titus 3:5, NIV 2011.
9. Gregory Smith. "About Three-in-Ten U.S. Adults Are Now Religiously
    Unaffiliated," December 14, 2021,
    https://www.pewresearch.org/religion/2021/12/14/about-three-in-ten-u-s-
    adults-are-now-religiously-unaffiliated/.

Chapter 11: Marriage

1. John Swartzwelder, "The Simpsons: Life on the Fast Lane," Season 1, Episode
    9, aired on March 18, 1990.
2. Genesis 1:27 and Romans 8:17, NIV 2011.

3. Jack Brewer, "ISSUE BRIEF: Fatherlessness and its effects on American society," May 15, 2023, https://americafirstpolicy.com/latest/issue-brief-fatherlessness-and-its-effects-on-american-society#:~:text=Across America, 2022 data indicates,are led by single mothers.

4. Nick Cady, "The Impact on Kids of Dad's Faith and Church Attendance," June 20, 2016, https://nickcady.org/2016/06/20/the-impact-on-kids-of-dads-faith-and-church-attendance/

5. Children's Bureau blog, "A Father's Impact On Child Development," May 12, 2023, https://www.all4kids.org/news/blog/a-fathers-impact-on-child-development/#:~:text=Many would admit that they,numb the pains of fatherlessness.

6. Acts 5:41, NIV 2011.

7. Ken Curtis, "What Happened to the Twelve Apostles?" April 28, 2010, https://www.christianity.com/church/church-history/timeline/1-300/whatever-happened-to-the-twelve-apostles-11629558.html

8. Genesis 2:18, NIV 2011. The Hebrew word translated "helper" can also have the idea of counterpart.

9. Luke 15:7, NIV 2011.

10. John 8:9-11, NIV 2011.

11. Matthew 18:21-35, NIV 2011.

12. Matthew 6:12, KJV 1987.

13. C.S. Lewis, *Mere Christianity*, (Touchstone Books, 1996).

14. Gary Chapman, "What are the Five Love Languages," https://5lovelanguages.com/learn.

15. Matthew 22:1-14, NIV 2011.

16. Isaiah 25:6, NIV 2011.

17. Revelation 21:1-27, NIV 2011.

Made in the USA
Las Vegas, NV
21 December 2023

83301683R00115